AN ACT OF CONSCIENCE

An Act of Conscience

by Len Holt

BEACON PRESS   BOSTON

The author gratefully acknowledges permission to reprint passages from *The Dream Keeper* by Langston Hughes, copyright 1932 by Alfred A. Knopf, Inc., New York, reprinted by permission of the author; "Remembering Nat Turner" by Sterling A. Brown; "Epistrophe" by LeRoi Jones, published in *The Beat Scene* by Elias Wilentz and Fred McDurrah (Corinth Books, Inc., 1960); "If We Must Die" by Claude McKay, published in *Selected Poems of Claude McKay* (Bookman Associates, Twayne Publishers, Inc.); and passages from the unpublished poems of Julian Bond and Dawley, by permission of the authors.

Acknowledgments

Gratitude is expressed to the following people in connection with this book:

Howard Zinn, who used a teacher's gift of encouragement. Pete Beveridge, who took time to evaluate the structure and philosophy of legalism contained in the book when employed as an adjunct of social protest.

My Mom Golden, who burned her fingers lighting candles for her son's success and who came to Danville with my brother, John, and an extra toothbrush—prepared to go to jail in her sixtieth year if it would help.

Thanks goes also to O. C. Thaxton, Essie Gordon, and A. D. McCain, who, along with the scholar Daniel Foss, generously gave me access to their clippings and notes; and to Casey Gurewitz and Dawn Lander for technical assistance.

Recognition must go to Joseph A. Jordan and Edward A. Dawley, my former law partners, who spent six years trying to impart to me all of the practical things they knew about protecting the rights of the oppressed in the courtroom, and who made it possible for me to travel as an extension of them throughout the South, serving the legal needs of hundreds of indigents.

Thanks go to Jim Lee, an artist and businessman of note from Detroit, who ended all postponement on my part of writing the book and insisted I "tell it like it is." Appreciation is given to Bill Mahoney, who interrupted his own writing projects to give hours of help . . . and to Rita, whose life was disrupted most by the incessant pecking of a typewriter throughout the wee hours of the nights and mornings.

Finally, there is Miss Ella Josephine Baker, whose service to the cause of Americans of color has been second to none. Some years ago she was a popular girl orator with a booming contralto voice. During this period she molded some words into a poem which express part of her great spirit which has held so high the Freedom Banner:

> *Ask no mercy for my birth*
> *No pity for my skin*
> *I demand to be*
> *By right of worth*
> *A man in a world of*
> *Men.*

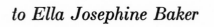

to Ella Josephine Baker

Contents

Author's Note

There are several books describing the heroics of protest against racism; but this book is more.

It's a discussion of the essence of a damned town, one that exists anywhere there is a smug white community convinced that it has done a great deal to "advance the welfare of our Negroes," or where there is a Negro community persuaded that the horrors of Mississippi and South Africa are a long way off.

Paradoxically, in the pages that follow, there is the greatness of little men as well as whatever pettiness there is to report of big men.

Herein are the struggles within the guts of a protest movement which sap more energy, corrode more spirits, and immobilize more "soldiers" than all the assassinations of Herbert Lees, Medgar Everses, Louis Allens, James Chaneys, Mickey Schwerners and Andrew Goodmans; than all the broken heads, split faces, filthy jails and the racists who preside over them.

This book asks: must the price of Freedom be so dear?

The vehicle for posing and answering this question is Danville, and the Danvilles are everywhere.

They exist in Chicago where politicians and *responsible* Negro leaders solicit door-to-door pledges not to participate in school boycotts; in New York where civil rights groups push purges of maverick leaders and sully their lips with formulations from City Hall; and in Cambridge, Maryland, where preachers call a lady named Richardson "godless."

Time is short for those of us who would "Redeem the Soul of America" because we must first find that soul.

Time is also short for us who have a date with Virginia *justice,* and possibly prison, under the same law used to send John Brown to the gallows: inciting the colored population to commit acts of "violence and war against the white population."

Significant numbers of us must engage in acts of conscience with a sense of urgency to reconstruct our America. This book describes one of the many starting points taken by some Americans to eliminate the problems of race which manifest themselves so discouragingly in places like Jackson . . . New York . . . Chicago . . . San Francisco . . . Danville.

AN ACT OF CONSCIENCE

CHAPTER 1

Yeah, Team!

Cheerleaders usually carry megaphones and wear decorated sweaters. I had neither in Danville. In place of a megaphone were lungs, which rendered some service. In place of a fancy sweater I wore a dark suit and a clip-on bow tie. Conventional cheerleaders perform at stadiums and gymnasiums. For me there were the Southern courts, where rare is the presiding judge—in either the state or the federal system—who can pronounce the word "Negro" without causing you to wonder if he didn't slip that time and say "nigger." Danville was no exception.

The Reverend Alexander I. Dunlap of Danville nicknamed me "Snake Doctor" after having read for a sermon Matthew 9:16 ". . . be ye therefore wise as serpents and harmless as sheep." I've never understood the connection, but it was a frightened Snake Doctor coming into Danville, Virginia, on a noisy Piedmont Airlines plane the morning of June 24, 1963, a Monday, at 9:00 A.M. I was returning from New York City, where I had conferred with Leonard Boudin, one of the top constitutional lawyers in America.

My stomach churned and my throat felt like a sandpit. There was an overwhelming desire to go to the bathroom or stay on the plane or to get anywhere except Danville. Three weeks earlier, June 6, 1963, my arrival in Danville had been different; I was much calmer. Mr. Julius Adams, Reverend Dunlap, and Reverend Lawrence G. Campbell had been arrested, and sent for me to defend them. These three men were considered "Movement" leaders—the "Movement" being the collective name for the organizations involved in Danville's protest against racial segregation as well as the name given to the act of protesting.

The plane landed. I got off, walking rapidly, cussing to myself to disguise the feeling a balloon must have in a pin factory. I was afraid of being shot.

Every policeman, state trooper, and prison farm guard knew me and hated me as "that smart nigger bastard who tries to make fools of white folks." There were a lot of these guys in and around Danville, because demonstrations were still a threat. If they wanted to take a shot they were in good shape as I got off that plane. Three days before, along with ten others including Reverend Dunlap, I had been indicted under the John Brown statute for inciting the colored population "to acts of violence and war against the white population" and had not been arrested yet. Legally my status was that of an indicted felon-at-large. "Resisting arrest" or "escaping arrest" were the magical phrases that officers could use if any explanation became necessary as to why I had been shot. The law was just that clear. The willingness of local officials to maim or injure had been demonstrated in Danville, behind the City Hall, two weeks earlier, on June 10, 1963. Women had been beaten between their thighs, on their buttocks and breasts; men and boys had had their bodies clubbed into numbness. On this date, two weeks later, there was still an abundance of bruises, shaven heads, and suppurating gashes.

"Snake Doctor!" Reverend Dunlap shouted as he ran from the terminal building toward me. I ran toward him. Pointing to a package, I said, "Lap, take this package. It's got the suit to be filed this morning which attacks the 'John

Brown' statute. If they get me before I get to the Court—I mean arrest me—make sure that this gets filed."

As we sprinted towards Dunlap's white 1962 Cadillac, two shriveled-looking white men in shirt sleeves moved from the shadows of the airport building with hands in pockets. As my heart stopped and my mouth flew open to scream, I recognized them: F.B.I. agents.

Dunlap had gone on, flung my luggage and the package containing the papers to be filed on his back seat, and was starting the motor while smiling at my fright. In seconds we were on the way to Danville, to the Post Office where the Federal Court under Judge Thomas J. Michie was in session.

Dunlap's full six-foot three-inch frame vibrated with laughter as he related, as only a black man could, "Snake Doctor, the white folks are going to catch hell this morning. All your boys are in town for the cases. And so is Tucker of the NAACP."

I wondered how the F.B.I. knew I would return this morning and on that flight; then I remembered that an Atlanta F.B.I. agent informed me in 1960 that it was their customary procedure to tap the phones used by those engaged in racial protest. "Do they give the segregationist the same attention?" I asked Dunlap.

"What?" he replied, not knowing what I was talking about. The gleaming machine shot to sixty miles per hour. Behind us, at the same speed, were the two F.B.I. agents in a 1962 chocolate brown Plymouth.

We stopped at the traffic light just beyond the underpass coming from the East on U.S. 58, a quarter of a mile from where the Danville City Prison Farm faces the highway. A black Cadillac pulled alongside, stopped; a light brown skinned, dapper man sprang from the car and hopped into the back of the Dunlap car. It was Andrew C. Muse, Danville civil rights lawyer.

"Here," he said as he thrust an official paper into my hand. "In the name of freedom for all black men, God and the United States, I hereby serve you with this subpoena requiring you to be in Federal Court within ten minutes," Muse recited pontifically.

I relaxed. At last some of the fright was dissipated. Somebody had used imagination and done some research. To make sure that I got to the Federal Court for the hearing this subpoena had been obtained for me to get me there as a witness. Muse served it because no federal marshals were available.

I soon learned what Dunlap meant when he said, "My boys were in town." There were lawyers from everywhere: Charles Beavers, Arthur Kinoy, and William Kunstler of New York; Shelley Bowers, Professor Chester Antieu and three research law students from the District of Columbia; Dean Robb of Detroit; Miss Ruth Harvey, Jerry Williams, Harry I. Wood, George Woody, S. W. Tucker, and Andrew C. Muse of Virginia.

Between Friday, June 21, and Monday, June 24, the date of trial, this interracial legal corps had assembled in Danville, organized, divided the work, marshalled witnesses and evidence, and was ready for battle. They were a heartening sight for Danville Negroes, one of whom commented, "How can we lose with God and that 'bar association' sitting there on our side?" Unfortunately, the federal judge wasn't.

Judge Thomas Jefferson Michie of the United States District Court for the Western District of Virginia is a patient, plumpish, jowled, kindly person who would be cast on television as the friendly family doctor. He is a member of the Virginia aristocracy whose family in Charlottesville traces its ancestry back to Captain John Smith of Jamestown and Pocahontas. He's reputed to be a multimillionaire. Prior to his federal judgeship appointment by President Kennedy in 1961, he served on the city council of Charlottesville, the site of the University of Virginia.

As a judge he is methodical and slow—almost as if unsure. He is consistent, though. His decisions are as predictable as those of Judges Mize and Cox, federal judges in Mississippi.

We didn't know it at the time of the June 24 trial, but the aggressive program of legal counterattack to the hellishness of Danville justice would soon embarrassingly push Judge Michie into a corner unliked by congenial southerners: the corner of choice between the past and the present.

Danville sensed the importance of the issues before the Danville Federal Court that day. Would the United States be on the side of black men fighting racism or on the side of those who had hosed, beaten, and jailed the singers of "We Shall Overcome"?

Black Danville served notice it considered the hearing important. It filled all seats and aisles in the courtroom and overflowed into the hall. Danville's power structure gave its own recognition. Cops—in and out of uniform—repeatedly photographed the individual members of the battery of civil rights lawyers. These civil rights lawyers were followed because city officials were frightened. There was reason for the fright.

F.B.I. agents had been gathering pictures and interviewing the brutality victims of the cops, garbage men, and taxi drivers who had used newly issued, blonde clubs for the carnage of June 10. The F.B.I. was an unknown factor—then. Would the investigation lead to federal criminal prosecution of policemen and city officials under 42 U.S.C. 241-

242* for the crushed skulls and split faces—or would the reports get the "File 13" treatment?

Judge Michie was also an *unknown.* Would the outrages of Danville so anger Judge Michie as to cause the power of the Federal government to be invoked against Danville in righteous indignation? Would these outrages alter the pattern of his past decisions?

The five specific questions before the federal court were:

1. Would Danville be allowed to continue cutting off unemployment compensation to all persons arrested for demonstrations who fought the charges instead of pleading guilty?
2. Would Danville be allowed to continue to use an invalid anti-picketing ordinance to arrest integration demonstrators?
3. Was the Danville Corporation Court's anti-racial demonstration injunction† valid?
4. Would the 105 demonstrators be permitted to have the charges of violating the Danville injunction tried in federal court under 28 U.S.C. 1443‡ or be remanded back to Judge A. A. Aiken and the Danville Corporation Court?
5. Would the federal court stop arrests and prosecutions of those indicted for inciting the colored population "to acts of violence and war" (John Brown law, Va. Code 18. 1-422), until such time as a three-judge District Court could be convened under 28 U.S.C. 2281 and pass upon the validity of the Virginia statute?

* For full text of these sections of the U.S. Code, see p. 229.
† For full text, see pp. 230–231.
‡ For full text, see p. 231.

Only the fourth question was allowed extensive production of evidence that day, June 24, 1963. Here the Movement lawyers had the dual burden of showing that the demonstrators were arrested merely for engaging in peaceful exercise of First Amendment rights and that no fair trial could be had in Danville's Corporation Court.

The courtroom was warm and stuffy; the air conditioning, if any existed, was not designed for the overload this hearing had brought forth. I exchanged greetings with almost every black face between the courtroom door and the twenty-four seats placed around the table for the plaintiffs' lawyers—for once we were the plaintiffs, the attackers in Danville legal affairs.

Sitting where a jury normally sat were reporters, Chief Eugene McCain of the Danville Police, and a few of his lesser officers, along with Alan G. Marer of the Justice Department. In his hand was a yellow legal pad ready for note-taking, and even though the proceedings had not started he was writing and intermittently tossing his head to throw back a wild lock of black hair off the lens of his horn-rimmed glasses. Marer was the third Justice Department man to come to Danville. The other two had come, taken notes, and left. I had made it a point to ride hard on Marer, who always seemed to be at the office of Harvey and Wood, where the Movement lawyers prepared for the endless trials. "Man, do you think those people downtown are going to be impressed with more notes? Why don't you guys in the government do something? Betcha when the world comes to an end, you'll be sitting around to take notes to file on top of some of those other big piles of papers in Washington."

Marer never replied in kind to my jabbing, and only once did his face flush from anger. It was then that I was glad I hadn't carried my criticism of the inaction of the Justice Department further.

Swallowed by the sea of black people and their lawyers were two lone figures sitting at the defense counsel table: James H. Ferguson, the City Attorney for Danville, and John Carter, city councilman and the publicly identified leader of those running Danville, who believed that the way to end the integration protests was never to show the "softness" of "Bull" Connor's Birmingham police. Off to the side of Carter and Ferguson was the Commonwealth Attorney of Danville and the Attorney General of Virginia, Robert Y. Button.

"All rise," shouted the United States Marshall. He pounded the gavel, silencing the courtroom as United States District Judge Thomas Michie walked in from his chambers and took his place on the bench standing before his upholstered chair. The federal court hearing had begun.

The fight was on . . . and this time we hoped and believed—in spite of experiences to the contrary—that God and the United States were on our side. How unlike the feeling Negroes have when they go into a state court. Perhaps a partial explanation for this attitude is that Negroes in America (rightly or wrongly) do view the white community as a sort of god and themselves as a Job.

The Bible relates how God in a game with the devil allowed Job to be inflicted with flesh-eating worms and other diseases to see if Job would abandon God and curse him. Jod didn't. Negroes often have a similar attitude. No matter how heinous the acts of one set of white persons, hope is maintained; the search goes on for the white person down the road who will repudiate his brothers' injustice.

Danville Negroes knew how they had been beaten, denied, crushed, and castrated in spirit over the years. They could not forget the beatings of the peaceful demonstrators behind the Danville City Hall only fourteen days before, on June 10, 1963; bandages and scars were in evidence in the federal court that morning. They also knew about the procedures of the Danville Corporation Court. But today for Negroes things would be different; the federal court was in session. That day Judge Michie was the United States of America, the Constitution, the President, Abraham Lincoln, Franklin D. Roosevelt, the United States Army, and John Brown, all in one bundle.

The trial began. Sam W. Tucker, representative of the Legal Defense Fund of the NAACP and chairman of the Legal Redress Committee of the Virginia State Branches of the NAACP, opened the case.

"May it please the court." Tucker's voice pierced the stillness of the chamber. He arranged his notes on the yellow pad and rays of sunlight coming in from the windows to his left danced over his brown and balding head.

Meticulously he set forth the statute under which the proceedings were being held as Title 28 U.S.C. 1443, and indicated that the Negro plaintiffs felt they were entitled to the protection of the federal government from the oppressive hand of Danville officials under both subsections of that statute, in that no fair trial could be had in Danville's Corporation Court.

"We think that the evidence in this case is going to show that the Negro citizens in Danville follow the usual type of things by which people seek to be redressed of their grievances: petitions to government authorities, by conferences, by all sorts of means, but have received the same deaf ear.

"So that by necessity they were driven to make the point known, to call attention not only to the authorities of Danville but the attention of the entire State, Nation and the world of the fact that here yet—notwithstanding the Constitutional doctrine change—the authority of State power in Danville is still being used to maintain what was the situation under the *Ferguson Doctrine*."

Tucker's voice became emotional, the pitch raised, and a little of the horror scream of those beaten on the night of June 10 crept into it. Both of his hands reached forward as if to strangle.

"But there is an end to negotiation! An end to petitioning! There is an end—there is a time when action is required! Somewhere there is a limit as to how long *Freedom* in its complete sense can be denied persons!"

"Tell it!" came from several throats in the middle aisle. Lowering his pitch, Tucker continued.

"This country cannot deny that. That was the spirit that moved the Thirteen Colonies in *revolt* against the mother country. So that another step was taken: direct action."

Tucker's voice rippled on, describing the near success of negotiation between Movement leaders and several of the Danville city councilmen after early demonstrations were rendered abortive when forces led by John Carter, now sitting across from Tucker, had refused even token concession to Danville Negroes. Carter's face turned crimson.

Tucker went on to describe June 10, a day of "infamy to the fair name of Virginia," when the helpless women with a scattering of men were knocked down with hundreds of pounds of pressure from fire hoses, surrounded by Danville police and beaten with new clubs. He then turned his attention and that of the Court and the hundreds of spectators to the injunction issued by Judge Aiken of the Corporation Court which banned First Amendment rights of Danville Negroes, and to the trials held under that injunction on June

17 and 18, 1963, in spite of the transfer of those cases to the federal court:

> Trials conducted in the state court as a result of general warrants being made up on mimeographed forms and passed out to police officers to go and arrest whomever you please—"just fill in the name."
>
> Trials for violating a blanket injunction which can be taken as enjoining all sorts of activities without even any specification as to what any one individual on trial is alleged to have done in violation of the injunction.
>
> Trials conducted without any showing of proof, or proof that the defendant on trial had notice or knowledge of the injunction. Trials held in an atmosphere of a police state where people are searched on their entry to the courtroom.

On and on Tucker went, setting forth the scores of facts which had rendered those trials little more than naked displays of brute power by Danville, including such evidence as the Judge's reading of a previously prepared statement which could only have been typed before the trial, as he sentenced the defendants and in effect denied their right to appeal by keeping them in jail, so their time would have been served before the Virginia Supreme Court could hear the cases months later.

Tucker concluded and took a seat among the score of plaintiff lawyers, self-consciously aware of the stillness of the courtroom.

The statement had been longer and more emotional than called for by the technical posture of the law. We had no jury, only Judge Michie, to convince. Emotional appeals aren't supposed to be made to judges. But we were glad that Tucker had done it exactly as he had. The more than eight

hundred spectators, most of whom were Negroes, needed to
"hear the message." Up to that point there had been nothing
but jailings, beatings, shootings, and the crushing of spirits.
At last their day was coming; the federal government was
now involved.

The courtroom was quiet, almost drowsy with heat after
the spell created by Tucker's peroration. On the far wall the
patterns of shadows thrown by the slatted blinds were climb-
ing diagonally. Languidly the marshal got up from his seat,
picked up a black leather-bound Bible, and waited in front
of the witness stand.

A dapper young man wearing a sport coat and summer
slacks, whose handsome, olive-tan features were accentuated
by a neatly trimmed mustache, moved toward the marshal.
The witness was the Reverend Lawrence George Campbell
of Danville's Bibleway Holiness Church.

As the Reverend Campbell was being sworn in, Harry
I. Wood quietly stood brushing back the fold of his coat,
concentrated his massive frame over the notes before him.
Wood was one of the five Negro lawyers practising in Danville. All of them had, at great personal risk, defied the *big
mules* who run Danville and had created some strains on
their relationship with the NAACP by proceeding to serve
the Movement.

Reverend Campbell sat in the elevated witness chair,
crossed his legs, and locked his fingers together over the top
of one knee. He exuded confidence, and was clearly accustomed to speaking in public.

In a brisk, businesslike manner, Wood took Campbell
through the formal preliminaries. Campbell was a local
minister and First Vice-President of the Danville Christian
Progressive Association, which was in control of the Move-

ment and which was an affiliate of Martin Luther King's
Southern Christian Leadership Conference (SCLC).

Reverend Campbell told how the demonstrations had
begun in Danville on May 31, with those in the demonstrations receiving admonitions to be nonviolent. Demonstrators
were searched for weapons: "We asked if they had any
weapons on them, namely perhaps a knife, fingernail file,
pencil or pen or anything that might inflict a wound on any
individual." In describing the first demonstration Campbell
emphasized that the police didn't protect those in the line of
march from cars although the group had a parade permit.

He pointed out that the Negroes in Danville had been
petitioning the city hall over a period of many years for im-
provements. Failing to get satisfaction in this way, the minister stated, demonstrations began "to get . . . Negro representation in the Board of Plans and Commissions, secondly,
that they would give us desegregation of all public accommodations; in essence we would be entitled to all of the rights
that all of the citizens are entitled to."

As the Reverend Campbell proceeded smoothly through
his direct testimony, Alan G. Marer's head of dark hair
bobbed furiously as his pen scampered across the pad.
Marer seemed especially interested in Campbell's remarks as
to how the demonstrations seemed to be producing results
after six days when a Danville City Councilman named
Womack had arranged negotiations and two meetings were
held. During one of the meetings, the one on June 7, Campbell and two other leaders were notified that they had been
indicted for allegedly inciting the colored population "to
acts of violence and war against the white population."

Campbell's testimony revealed a facet of the minor
struggle among the powers that ran Danville. One faction

was willing to make some concessions. The other one wasn't
—and it was in control.

Nat Conyers and Dean Robb, two volunteer lawyers
from the National Lawyers Guild who were serving the
Movement, had been assigned to anticipate what defense the
City would pose. The demonstration in the Mayor's office
was one which had been anticipated.

Reverend Campbell described the demonstration:

"We were on the steps of the courthouse and all of us
turned around and went into the Municipal Building to the
Mayor's office. There we sat and sang. About 5:30 or there-
abouts, Chief McCain said that it was time for the offices to
close and that we had to go. And we told him—I told him
that we did not intend to go, that we wanted to have an
audience with the Mayor, the City Manager. And at this
particular point they grabbed me by my arms and dragged
me through the corridor and carried me to the elevator.
There is where I saw an officer hit one of our demonstrators.
No one was armed or anything and he hit him and knocked
him up against the elevator and I told Captain Boswell:
'Don't you see that officer hitting that boy' and he said to
me 'I don't see him because I am looking at you.' "

Blood surged to my face. Murmurs around me and behind me indicated a similar emotion among the hundreds of
Negroes in the courtroom. The flitting eyes of Chief McCain
of the Danville police darted over the shoulder of Alan
Marer of the Justice Department to his note pad. The brutality of the police was fresh enough to evoke intense responses.

After a preliminary question showed that Reverend
Campbell only saw the start of the June 10 night march, the
lawyer, Harry Wood, directed Campbell: "Well, describe it
up to that point."

"On June 10 we were at the Bibleway Church and we had a mass meeting there and of course we sang . . . and then people volunteered to go down to the jail and to walk around the jail and to sing. The purpose of this was to manifest their disapproval of the injustice that had been imposed upon our people and of course we thought maybe about fifty would turn out—perhaps there may have been more— I am not certain, but they left the church at this point. I remained at the church and Reverend McGhee led the demonstration."

"What was your observation of this group, when they left the church, regarding order and ordinances?" Lawyer Wood asked.

"They were very orderly in that Reverend McGhee had informed them that night to do the same thing we had instructed them to do. We had prayer and the people gathered in the street. The reason I say that they were orderly was because everyone took particular time to get in maybe twos or threes, maybe perhaps three abreast, and we took time to get a car to follow behind us to give light so that any vehicle coming down Industrial Avenue might recognize or notice the light that was shining. They were orderly."

With precision, James A. Ferguson, Danville City Attorney, began the cross-examination.

In contrast to the procedure of the plaintiff attorneys, Ferguson sat at the dark mahogany table. He bored into Campbell, using a high-pitched voice rendered more rasping by a heavy nasal twang.

Ferguson forced Campbell to give almost entirely "yes" and "no" answers:

"Did you see any of your group in the middle of the street shaking cars side to side?" Ferguson asked, referring to earlier demonstrations.

"Yes, I saw a fellow push a car, yes I did." Campbell answered. Ferguson got Campbell to state that the demonstrators had carried a coffin with a sign on it saying "Segregation is dead," that they had sung in the Mayor's office during business hours, that some demonstrators had bottle caps while in the office, that they had sat on the floor, had yelled "Segregation is Dead," had refused to leave the office, and had blocked traffic on the street by sitting down.

Ferguson's questions came in a rapid staccato; Judge Michie seemed impressed; Marer of the Justice Department wrote even more furiously; and I squirmed.

When I attempted to get up and object two arms pulled me down, those of Arthur Kinoy and Andrew Muse. "We've planned all this. We've got a united legal team. Just listen for once." Kinoy admonished me. Without further outward resistance I remained seated.

Inwardly I was disturbed. I was accustomed to participating freely. While I had been away over the weekend and the Danville Police were seeking me for my second arrest in Danville, Arthur Kinoy and William Kunstler had come to Danville and pushed the idea of all the lawyers uniting under one banner to defend the Movement and prepare a joint effort for this hearing. Jerry Williams of Danville had been made the director of the Committee.

Prior to the formation of the Committee, I had helped with the directing and planning of the legal moves and offered a number of suggestions to the other attorneys. I represented over 100 of the 150 people arrested up to that point, I was devoting full time to the Movement work while the other local attorneys had not abandoned all other practice, I had closest ties with the Movement leaders, and I had shown myself to have resources which could bring other attorneys into Danville to lend a hand.

But unity was good. The team assembled was impressive. Professor Chester J. Antieu of Georgetown Law School sat in front next to Shelly Bowers of the Washington, D.C., bar. Behind them was Dean Robb of the Michigan Bar who had left Detroit the week before to come to Danville under the auspices of the National Lawyers Guild Committee for Legal Assistance to the South (CLAS) after just having settled a personal injury case for $175,000. To Robb's right was William Kunstler of New York, who is among the best known American lawyers because of his extensive and creative work in civil rights litigation. At Kunstler's elbow was his partner and anchor man, Arthur Kinoy. Kinoy is affectionately known as the "Little General," partially because of his short fragile size, but more because of his agile mind and dramatic pyrotechnics before trial and appellate courts which put fire into dull and obscure legal postures. Here was a team that could lick hell out of any lawyers in the South, or lawyers from the North that the South could hire—if presented with fair judges.

And undergirding this team with the solid work that makes it easier for a star halfback to make an end run were the five Negro lawyers of Danville: Miss Ruth Harvey, Jerry Williams, Harry I. Wood, George Woody, and Andrew C. Muse.

Finally the tortuous cross-examination of Campbell ended.

A chubby lawyer on my right, Phil Hirschkop, who had handled the interviewing of the fifty persons who had marched from the Bibleway Church on the night of June 10 —only three of whom escaped without injuries—handed me the trial brief. Listed next as a witness, to my surprise, was the Reverend Doyle Thomas. Thomas was completely and totally orientated toward the NAACP and had been presi-

dent of the Danville chapter for the last four years. (In protest against the inaction of the Danville NAACP, the leaders
of the Movement had broken away in 1960, affiliated with
Martin Luther King's SCLC, and begun filing suits and
demonstrating.)

Speaking with a measured cadence befitting the image
of himself that he liked to project, Reverend Thomas re-
counted how five of the six entrances to the City Hall of
Danville (which contained all of the courts) were sealed
off; how at the one entrance left open on June 17 and 18,
1963, there were deputized garbage truck drivers serving as
guards who freely permitted white persons to enter while
making each Negro prove immediate and urgent necessity
for entrance; how the steps within the building were blocked
off and closed; and how more deputized garbage truck
drivers were running the elevators in place of the Negro
ladies who ordinarily performed this function. He also
described the armed camp atmosphere arising from the near
total attendance of the 75-man Danville Police force plus
scores of Virginia State Troopers at each of the court hearings dealing with the hundred Negroes charged with violating the injunction issued June 6, 1963, banning racial demonstrations.

All of us wanted Reverend Thomas to "whale," "blow,"
and get dramatic and emphatic as he characteristically did
on Sunday while delivering sermons at the Loyal Baptist
Church of Danville. If our desires were known to him, he
didn't respond. In a subdued voice he related key facts. Yet
he was effective. Sensing this pattern, Andrew Muse directed
the testimony, as calmly as when he had served me with the
subpoena several hours earlier, orchestra fashion, using his
voice as a baton.

After showing that Reverend Thomas had been stopped

before going into the Danville Corporation Court, Muse paused, walked back to the counsel table, and fumbled with some papers. Suddenly pivoting, he asked: "Were you asked any questions after you were stopped?"

"No, no questions; he informed me that I had to be searched," Reverend Thomas replied. The black audience murmured. Reverend Thomas' voice grew stronger and the rest of his testimony grew livid with his personal anger. Indignation was obvious as he told how only Negroes were searched and that Negro women, including Ruth Harvey, the Negro attorney, were roughly searched. The fire in him had been unleashed.

When Judge Aiken's order in the Corporation Court requiring the searching was introduced as evidence, even the snarling voice of John Carter didn't perturb Reverend Thomas. Muse continued conducting his one-man symphony of Danville injustice.

"Did you notice anything unusual about the appearance of Judge Aiken at this time?" Muse inquired.

Pausing and slowly turning to stare into the eyes of the federal judge, Judge Michie, Reverend Thomas replied, "I noticed that he was wearing a gun."

Pressing in for all he was worth, Muse asked, "To your knowledge is it customary for him to wear a gun in Court?"

Before Reverend Thomas could part his lips, Judge Michie intervened in a tone of chastisement of Muse, "I don't think you need ask that question."

Time stood still a little.

Hundreds of pairs of eyes bored into Judge Michie's face. A second look was being taken as if to make sure that this was the Abraham Lincoln, Franklin D. Roosevelt, John Brown, John F. Kennedy government that had spoken. The audience seemed restless for the first time.

To the credit of both, John Carter and James Ferguson, who were handling the case for the City of Danville, avoided asking more than a few insignificant questions of Reverend Doyle Thomas.

But something had changed. On the far wall of the courtroom the pattern of lights and shadows of the sun coming through the window was gone; things weren't as bright; outside the clouds had cut off the rays of light.

In preparation for the testimony of the fourth witness, Mrs. Gloria Campbell, the wife of the Reverend Lawrence Campbell who had testified earlier, the Reverend Hildreth McGhee was placed on the stand and skillfully led through his testimony by William Kunstler of New York.

McGhee had led the march to the jail on the night of June 10, 1963, and had been arrested while praying. Mrs. Campbell had been among the forty-seven of the fifty marchers who had suffered injuries.

With great detail Reverend McGhee described the care used in removing weapons, limiting the number of marchers, avoiding obstructing traffic and securing the commitment of nonviolence from the night marchers, who were mostly ladies, and who sang in hushed tones, "Jesus Keep Me Near the Cross," allowing the Danville police to trap them in an eleven-foot corridor between the jail and City Hall. On one end of the corridor were the policemen. Quickly moving behind them at the other end of the corridor were firemen with hoses that spewed forth water under 700 pounds of brick-tearing force. Sam Tucker, in the opening statement of the trial, had called it "Danville's night of infamy."

Reverend McGhee got off the witness stand smiling at having testified and gone through a meaningless, snarling cross-examination by John Carter, the Danville City Councilman.

Mrs. Campbell's eyes appeared grayish brown and her face seemed never to have smiled as she took the stand. So obvious was her anger and so intense was her determination that one didn't consider her striking beauty: a shapely body and a delicately formed face without the faintest hint of wrinkles that would tell her age and minus all facial cosmetics, in keeping with the doctrine of the Holiness sect of Christianity which was an integral part of her life.

Fittingly, the examination of Mrs. Campbell was done by Miss Ruth Harvey, a petite yet full woman who had become a good lawyer without feeling that she had to "out-man men" in the process.

After the preliminaries, Miss Harvey led Mrs. Campbell to the details of the night of June 10, the events of which were almost sufficient to convince the strongest atheist that there is a God by reminding them that in spite of a thousand blows by muscular arms on vital and intimate parts of the bodies of women and boys, and water projected under neck wrenching force, no one died.

Mrs. Campbell gave the story: "When we arrived in this alley between the City Hall and the jail I was on the second row. We sang, 'Jesus Keep Me Near the Cross' and after we had gotten in this alley a long line of police formed between the City Hall and the jail.

"At this point the Reverend McGhee said, 'Let us now bow our heads and pray.' He prayed aloud and alone. At this point I saw police come to Bob Zellner and smash his camera and arrest him. Then I saw police go to Reverend McGhee and arrest him while he was still praying. Our group was silent."

So intense was the attention of the courtroom that one might have heard a paper clip drop. Anger hung in the air like a blanket. Mrs. Campbell didn't pause.

"At this time I heard a voice saying 'I am tired of you people! I have told you to stay away! Let them have it!'

"Then I heard loud laughter.

"At this time I saw a fire truck pull up the street about fifty feet and I saw the fire hoses being unwound out in the street. It was a most horrible moment to wait for the water to hit us. All of a sudden a great force of water hit me from my back and I was thrown to the pavement. Water was shot up my clothes. I was lying out on the pavement with my dress over my head. As I tried to get up I was beaten on my back by a policeman.

"We saw policemen standing all around us with long night sticks. They looked as if they had never been used before.

"I saw bodies washed under parked cars just as trash runs down a street after a hard rain.

"I heard horrible sounds. Screams like people were being burned up in a fire, the sounds were. As I tried to get up I was beaten in my back. I was helped out to the sidewalk by Mrs. Myrtle McLeod.

"As we got down in front of the A&P Supermarket, Mr. Don Smith's car was parked there and he was in it and he let me get in the car, and as many demonstrators as could also got in the car. We turned around, heading back to the Bibleway Church.

"A policeman was still running after the car. At this point the red light caught us right at the A&P. We stopped at the light. The policeman was still running after the car. We were afraid to go through the red light because that would be a violation. We were afraid to wait on the green light.

"The officer yelled at us: 'Go on through the red light and get out of here!' and at this point we went on back to

Bibleway Church. I saw that many had been wounded. Someone with a pickup truck had picked up a truckload of people who looked like butchered cattle with bloody, torn, clothes. And cars had helped people away.

"When I got to the church my husband carried me to the hospital in someone else's car and when I got to the hospital I saw heads that had been busted open. I saw people lying on stretchers and I saw people brought in by ambulances who were unconscious. Some had been given artificial respiration and oxygen."

Time stood still again. Mrs. Campbell paused. Miss Harvey paused. The score of lawyers pressing the cause of the Danville Negroes were motionless, but were staring into the eyes of Judge Michie. It was as if a look at one of the Danville policemen in the courtroom might result in leprosy. The lawyers for the city fidgeted with some papers and in a moment or so . . . the trance was broken.

After a few more questions about the extent of Mrs. Campbell's injuries from the hosing and beating, such as impaired hearing and elongated purple bruises over her body, the direct examination ended.

John Carter, City Councilman and lawyer, attempted to discredit Mrs. Campbell's accuracy, but wisely cut short the cross-examination after realizing that further questions would just pile on more details of horror.

All during the testimony the attorney from the Justice Department, Marer, continued his note-taking.

Wilson B. Waddy, an F.B.I. agent, gave testimony that the demonstrations he had witnessed were essentially peaceful and orderly and Mrs. Marie Carey testified that it was the Chief of Police McCain who had been the one beating Mrs. Campbell.

After two more witnesses who reinforced the testimony given earlier, I was called to take the stand.

Though asked simple questions, my answers were long and complex. In detail I gave lists of facts about things present or absent in the Corporation Court of Danville where the demonstrators were being tried—and whose cases had been removed to this federal court—which stripped all but the most remote vestige of due process from the trials: arrest without sworn warrants, search of attorney papers, armed atmosphere, no particulars, denial of jury trial, invalidity of the injunction, suspension of the rules of evidence, prejudgment of the cases, lack of notice, illegal coercion to abandon right to trial, denial of the right to appeal by reason of the right to bail, and other diverse complaints.

To John Carter again fell the task of cross-examination. To his credit he had the good sense again to end abruptly when it became apparent that his questions were only providing me with an opportunity to argue with him. Wisely, he asked no questions about the proceedings or lack of procedures at the Corporation Court.

In a surprise move (to all except those who had copies of the trial brief of the Movement lawyers), we rested our case. It was then the turn of the City of Danville to come forward and justify the injunction against the protest movement, the absence of a façade of fairness in the trials, the unleashing of the flailing arms of white cops, and white deputized garbage collectors, armed with clubs, on the bodies of persons such as Mrs. Campbell on the night of June 10.

In all three tasks Danville failed.

CHAPTER 2

The Gun

Marvel at the contradictions of our lives:
  —Injustice is done in the name of morality
  —Good is done for the wrong reasons.

                    —"The Wisdom of Dawley"

Not to be found was a power that would have compelled Judge Archibald M. Aiken of the Danville Corporation Court to come to that hearing on June 24, 1963, on the second floor of the Danville Post Office. Judges are judges—mighty men, near gods. Any subpoena issued by the Negro plaintiffs to bring Judge Aiken into federal court could have been quashed because federal judges hesitate to force state judges to submit to federal subpoenas. Aiken had come on his own.

Judge Aiken sat on the stand with the long shape of his kindly face accentuated by a bald head ringed with silver hair. He wore a tasteful dark blue suit, and the paunch acquired from more than sixty-five years of life on the good side was hardly noticeable.

With a nod the United States District Judge for the Western District of Virginia, Thomas J. Michie, acknowledged the presence of his friend. John W. Carter handled the direct examination of the Judge.

Fully expecting the Judge to deny the facts stated about his conduct of trials, the hundreds of black spectators and their lawyers waited.

Matter-of-factly Judge Aiken told how the Danville Corporation Court injunction was issued on his personal knowledge about conditions in Danville. The attorneys around me looked at each other in amazement; how could a judge freely admit that he was both judge and witness to the facts of an injunction, knowing that it could be proven that he had presided over trials and sentenced people to jail, without bail, after searching their lawyers and doing all the other things which had been done? How could he admit this?

Theoretically the law requires that judges be impartial. In furtherance of this fiction the legal rules demand that a judge who is witness to an event excuse himself from presiding over the trial of someone arrested in that event. Judge Aiken continued testifying.

"They were jumping, hollering, and cheering," Aiken related. "I believe that one time that day, I wouldn't be positive of it, but I think that one time during the day I had been to the clerk's office, where I could see what they were doing, and they sang a very beautiful hymn, 'Sweet Hour of Prayer.' They sang that, then they begun to holler and jump around."

In complete forthrightness Judge Aiken went on, and on, about each demonstration that he had observed. Then we were in for another surprise. He told how his dinner one evening had been interrupted by a call from the police department. They wanted him to come out to a demonstration where the streets were blocked. Upon his arrival at the scene of the demonstration the Judge testified that he told Reverend Campbell, "Reverend Campbell, you ought to break up this meeting here." And after some further exchange of words, Judge Aiken told Campbell, "I order you to break up this meeting and break up the crowd. He [Campbell] said, 'Well, I'm not going to do it.' I said all right, that's all I have to say to you and I turned and walked away. Chief McCain was there with me and *I told him I thought the thing to do was to arrest the leaders there and I believed the children would break up and go on away."*

There is only one judge, Judge Aiken, and only one court, the Danville Corporation Court, for the trial of criminal and civil matters in Danville once those matters have progressed beyond the police court level. Judge Aiken ordered the arrest of persons over whose trials he was destined to preside.

From the voice and manner of Judge Aiken it was apparent that he wasn't accustomed to ordering Negroes to do something and having those Negroes tell him, as was done here, "I'm not going to do it!"

By now, Alan G. Marer of the Justice Department had sheets of yellow paper full of notes folded over in front of him like leaves of a giant cabbage. John W. Carter conducted the examination in the deferential tone one might use to question a god.

"Judge Aiken, some comment has been made in this court about the fact that when these contempt hearings were being held you were wearing a revolver. Will you tell us the reason for that?"

"I didn't wear any revolver on the bench Mr. Carter. I wore it in a holster going home at night and coming to work in the morning. As soon as I got to my office I took it off and I did not wear my revolver on the bench."

"Why did you feel it necessary to carry a revolver going to and from work?"

"I wore it simply for protection."

"Did you have any information that threats had been made toward you?"

"No *direct* threats had been made, Mr. Carter. No direct

threats. I was advised by the Police Department that I might be on the spot along with other officials here. The Assistant City Manager came to my office the first thing one morning and said that he wanted to install lights around my home so that it would be well lighted in that vicinity at night. I was informed that I had better be on the lookout and police protection was assigned me around the clock. There is a police officer here with me right now."

Sincerity rang from all his statements: a fragile, old, white man, himself a judge and the son of a judge, who lived alone with his aged wife, had been told, by people whom he trusted, that his life was in danger.

Matching the delicateness of John W. Carter in handling the direct examination, William M. Kunstler of our team began the cross-examination. No need to make any tempers rise; here was a judge as a witness who was telling the truth, and, as in most civil rights cases, the truth was the deadly weapon needed by us to prevail. No, nothing must put Judge Aiken on the defensive, we all knew—just let him talk.

And talk Judge Aiken did.

He admitted that the final statement and speech at the first trial on June 17, 1963, which included the determination of guilt, the sentence, and the denial of bail, had been prepared in advance of the trial. He admitted that he maintained racial signs in the jury room of the courtroom, where the Negro juror—if by some error a Negro got on the jury—was directed to use the "colored" toilet. In full anger Judge Aiken told how the demonstrators had ". . . jeered me."

Again, on cross-examination the Judge admitted he had received no direct threats of violence.

The next witness called by the City of Danville was their Chief of Police, Eugene G. McCain. But one's mind should linger on Judge Aiken's testimony. For purpose of oratory Negroes often speak of the "white folks" and conjure up one solid mass of white faces determined to protect their comfort from the poor and the black. As true as this may be—when measured by the resulting conditions—it tends to obscure another important fact: that the white powers and white leaders of a community are often divided as to method.

There are *violent whites,* convinced that the expeditious way to make sure that protest ends and Negroes slink away into invisibility is to take advantage of the first gathering of Negroes in protest, surround them, knock them down with high pressure hoses, split open a lot of skulls with clubs . . . and allow the sight of bloodied and brutalized bodies to preach a sermon of hellishness and horror in the Negro ghetto: maiming and death are the rewards of those who protest and disturb the comfortable.

Of course all of this will be done in the name of law and order—it makes no difference whether the city be Harlem, Brooklyn, Rochester, Chicago, Birmingham or Danville.

And then there are the *limited coercion whites.* The violent whites think of the riot guns, dogs, tanks, and clubs first. The limited coercion whites tend to place this form of violence somewhere further back than position number one. When there is a politically active business community, with a middle-class distaste for disorder and the stench of adverse publicity from displays of bruteness, some negotiating can be done.

Was it just coincidental that Reverend Campbell and the other leaders of the Movement were enjoined by a broad order of the Danville Corporation Court (where Judge Aiken presides) while attending a negotiating session with a city councilman and other leaders of the business community? Was it another coincidence that the same Negro leaders were indicted by the Danville Corporation Court grand jury while a second meeting was being conducted to dissolve some of the racial segregation of the community?

In both of these court operations Judge Aiken was the key. He had called for and issued the injunction against demonstrations, and he had convened the special grand jury which handed down the indictments of the Negro leaders. This was a function that only Judge Aiken could perform because he was the only judge of a court of record in the community.

By placing Judge Aiken before a group of demonstrators in the street and encouraging him to assume the cop's role and to give an order to disperse that would not be obeyed, *fate* had made certain Judge Aiken's ego would be sorely ruffled. By telling the Judge his life was in danger and that of his wife, *fate* made sure that the one judge in Danville with the power to enjoin and to cause indictments would understand the necessity for responding to the demands of the violent white leaders.

I hope *fate* is never so successful again.

Then Chief McCain took the stand in federal court on June 24, 1963. From him the team of lawyers for the Movement only expected the testimony of a *good cop*.

When a "good cop" testifies he is expected to show no emotions, and in fact to seem indifferent to why he's testifying: "I just did my duty as I saw it." Obvious facts—those that are well known and easily proven because the cop knows that the attorney has a picture showing him standing over the body of the fifteen-year-old boy with a smoking gun— are admitted and justified. Small concessions are made by a good cop allowing the accused to look good in some non-important incidental: "He was immaculately dressed and showed me courtesy when I arrested him." The concession enhances the impression of fairness, impartiality and "I-was-just-doing-my-sworn-duty-as-I-saw-it."

After taking the short walk from the jury box, Chief McCain sat in the witness chair crossing his long slender legs in navy blue trousers which made his height reach up to six feet. It was then that the spectator in the courtroom could see best the pear shape of his body that was swelling towards obese proportions and was crowned by a small face with small eyes and mouth that gave the appearance of a child's face pasted on the head of a man. The gold "Chief" badge on the grayish blue shirt of his uniform matched in color the gold badge on the cap he held in his hands. As he breathed rapidly, the gold badge on his chest moved up and down.

In the fatherly tones of one who had tried hard to give every consideration to an errant child, he began testifying under the gentle leading of James Ferguson, the Danville City Attorney.

Yes, the demonstrators were protected, but they just moved from one excess to another and his patience became exhausted when they moved one evening into the offices of the City Manager and began singing, shouting, and insisting on remaining until they got an audience, and that violence rose as non-demonstrators threw rocks which injured some of his men.

With equanimity and with measured tones, he described a scene of uncouthness on the part of several demonstrators who became enraged when all the police had done was to arrest, June 5, 1963, two of the leaders of the demonstration: Reverend Lawrence Campbell and Reverend Alexander Dunlap.

"Were they in the street at that time?"

"In the street and on the sidewalk both. Someone had

gone for the Reverend Chase and he approached at approximately the same time as the group. And I asked Reverend Chase if he would endeavor to subdue the crowd or quiet them or get them to go home. He did. They paid no attention to him."

I grew tense along with others in the courtroom who were familiar with the dynamics of this day. The Reverend Lendell W. Chase, (although President of the Danville branch of Martin Luther King's Southern Christian Leadership Conference) up to the date of this particular demonstration had not engaged in the public protest. He had in fact derided and castigated Campbell and Dunlap for the demonstrations. Along with the Reverend Doyle Thomas and some others, Chase had received "confidential word" that things would be worked out by negotiation. On making his first appearance in the streets as the tool of the police, the demonstrators called him an "Uncle Tom." To his credit, he later recognized that he had allowed himself to be used. He, his wife, and his children subsequently became Danville's most demonstrating family.

On the policeman went to deny ever striking anybody, or carrying a club on the night of June 10 and avowing that the only thing in his hand customarily at night was a flashlight.

On this last denial murmurs of disbelief rippled through the courtroom.

In keeping with the "I-was-just-doing-my-duty" projection, Chief McCain asserted that he had asked the fifty persons demonstrating with prayer and song around the jail on June 10 to disperse twice before the forceful dispersing took place. After further remarks indicating alleged attacks on police cars, Chief McCain and the City Attorney, James Ferguson, smugly pleased with themselves, ended the direct testimony. The cross-examination was handled by Jerry Williams.

The first telling blow on cross-examination occurred when Williams asked Chief McCain about the deputized policemen:

"How many special police have you deputized since this started?"

"There have been 175 employees of the city sworn in as special police officers."

"Are there any Negroes that were sworn in as police officers at this time?"

"Not during this period."

Judge Michie intervened at this point. "Now let's not fight the battle of segregation here—that's an entirely different question and has nothing to do with this suit," Michie reminded in a drawl.

The thrust and parry kept up between Jerry Williams and McCain as Jerry asked more questions important as foundations and some questions merely to confuse McCain, who tried to anticipate what would be asked next.

Unobtrusively Jerry Williams asked: "Is it customary for the police officer or anybody on the police force to report to you, or somebody in the police department, any people that are injured in the line of duty by these police officers?"

"It is customary that they report to me," the Chief responded.

"None of them reported to you after the night of June 10?"

"That's right."

"Did you see the police officers beating anybody out there that night of June 10 after the Council meeting?"

"I did not." Chief McCain replied with some anguish. We surmised he was embarrassed to say there were no reports, since there should have been, and if there were reports he did not want to be required to produce them for our inspection. The denial stirred the courtroom. A woman's voice asked: "Lord, how can he do it?"

Jerry Williams pressed the point. Showing by both facial expression and voice how incredible McCain's answer sounded, he asked again, "You didn't see *anybody* hit out there that night?"

In a desperate attempt to salvage his composure and the image that he wanted to present to Judge Michie, Chief McCain excitedly replied: "Other than myself. I was struck out there!"

For reasons I'll never know, Chief McCain didn't follow the standard guidelines. There were at least 300 persons in Danville ranging from the Mayor to deputized garbage truck drivers and Negro bootblacks who could place McCain at the scene of the beating. His own testimony placed him there, yet the only injury he personally witnessed was his own.

Of the 50 demonstrators, 47 were injured and treated at the segregated colored hospital. The fact that there were injuries could be proven by the injured persons, bystanders, and the personnel at the hospital, who had worked on a disaster schedule when the 47 persons suddenly flooded the small, 35-bed building. Yet Chief McCain had no reports of injuries inflicted by his men. Something had gone amiss.

There was a hurried and whispered conference between the two lawyers for the City of Danville and the Attorney General of Virginia, Robert Y. Button, before they announced: "We don't care to put on more witnesses."

Our side put on a short rebuttal consisting of Mrs. Mary Thomas, a twenty-four-year-old mother of two whose leg had been beaten and face smashed and broken by a police officer; without hesitation she pointed to Chief McCain as the one. And Dr. H. W. Harvey, the youngest of Danville's three Negro physicians, told about the persons injured on the night of June 10 and the treatment given. With the insertion into the federal court record of the transcripts of the two "trials" of demonstrators before Judge Aiken we rested our case, and Alan Marer of the Justice Department stopped writing on his yellow pad. Presentation of evidence had ended for the federal court hearing of June 24, 1963.

Getting into the streets, to demand that the white community take some minimal remedial steps to patch up some shabby conditions, is one of the Negro's most potent forms of *black insistence.* Desperation and hope are its parents. Desperation and hope had placed Danville's Movement lawyers in the federal court before Judge Michie.

There was desperation and there was hope with regard to the trials of hundreds of persons charged with violating the Corporation Court injunction. The desperation was born of the futility of trials before a judge who considered himself insulted by the demonstrators and who apparently believed that the demonstrators might be participants in a plot on his life. No wonder then the search of everyone black, the denial of bail to those convicted, the lack of particulars, the lack of a jury, the lack of an opportunity to challenge the very injunction under which people were being jailed without bail, and all the other things lacking which were, and are, considered essential for due process. This was our desperation.

Our hope was that Judge Michie would allow the cases to be removed from the state court under the provisions of 28 U.S.C. 1443 to remain in federal court and be tried or dismissed. William Kunstler had been pushing Federal Removal Action all over the country and hadn't prevailed yet. But we were hopeful because there had never been a case of a gun-toting judge under the conditions presented by Danville. Our hope was that Judge Michie would not send us back to Judge Aiken.

In desperation we had filed a federal suit for declaratory judgment that the injunction issued by Judge Aiken was invalid. Our expectations on this matter were almost on the level of cockiness. Professor Antieu of Georgetown Law School had looked at the injunction and laughed: "Any idiot freshman in law school can see that this is *less* than valid."

Even if Judge Michie had sent the cases back to the Corporation Court, his declaration that the injunction was invalid would have caused hundreds of charges to be dropped and thousands of dollars in bond money to be released and would have given a tired, beaten, and bruised Negro populace assurance that "God and the federal government were on our side."

There was also the matter of the Danville anti-picketing ordinance which was before the federal court at this hearing. It was worse than the state court injunction—if such be possible.

The thing that revealed most the truth that violence can be committed with a fountain pen was the cutting off of unemployment checks to arrested persons. Some of the persons arrested, who were not even demonstrating, but were swept up in a move to put everyone black in jail, had been receiving small unemployment checks with which they fed their families while waiting for the months to pass for the reopening of the tobacco factories. The checks were stopped. The State of Virginia took the position that to be eligible for unemployment checks you had to be able to work. Persons awaiting trials or appeals could never tell when they would have to go into court or go to jail, and, hence they were not "available" for work as the state defined it. The pressure existed for them to plead guilty to something, beg for mercy, and hope that the matter would end. The lawyers had filed a suit that was before Judge Michie at this hearing to stop the state from cutting off unemployment checks merely because a person had been arrested . . . to end punishment without guilt.

On the spot, and without hesitation, Judge Michie said "I'm not going to touch those unemployment matters."

The last matter before Judge Michie at the federal hearing was the revised *John Brown Statute* of Virginia, which now provided a minimum of five years' imprisonment and a maximum of ten years' imprisonment for inciting the colored population "to acts of violence and war against the white population." The fourteen of us indicted considered ourselves relatively lucky. Under the same law when John Brown was indicted, the punishment was death. This was the suit that I had brought into Danville with me earlier this same morning. It had been filed in the Clerk's Office of the United States District Court of Danville where the hearing was held while testimony was being taken; and most of the Danville and state officials named in the suit had been served with copies of it.

This federal suit attacked the constitutionality of the *John Brown* law and asked for immediate federal action stopping indictments and arrests under the law. Though indicted, James Forman, executive secretary of the Student Nonviolent Coordinating Committee (SNCC) and I had not yet been arrested under this law.

In chambers I pressed Judge Michie to use his federal power to issue a temporary restraining order stopping further indictments and arrests. I failed . . . with a small exception: Judge Michie asked that my arrest be postponed twenty-four hours in order to make me available, if needed, for the discussion among all the lawyers scheduled for the next day, Tuesday, June 25, 1963.

Wednesday night, June 26, about 11:00 P.M., one of several squad cars that followed me around stopped me after I had taken Attorneys Harry Lore and William Lee Akers of Philadelphia to the passenger depot of the Southern Railway. A short policeman with the neck of his shirt open came up to the window of the white Renault I was driving: "Are you Len Holt, the Snake Doctor?"

At first I didn't respond. I knew the cop wasn't serious about identification. For nearly an hour a week before I had waved my chubby brown finger in his face as the same cop had sweated and had been forced to admit he didn't know whether the demonstrators had been asked to move. Now I sweated. In Danville, as in all other American cities, I was an arrested person, a black man; and like it or not, my god was standing before me.

The impulse to tell him "I'm your mother!" had only a fleeting existence. I said nothing, just stared. I was being arrested for alleged incitement of Negroes to war against white people. Two other squad cars drove up and formed a huddle around me as a strong feeling surged that in spite of my desire to control myself, not to show fear, and to maintain under arrest the same arrogant posture I had given these cops when not under arrest . . . that at any moment I would piss. Minutes later, as a result of my second arrest in Danville within two weeks, I was in jail. (Fourteen days earlier, June 14, 1963, I had been arrested on a charge of violating Judge Aiken's Corporation Court injunction banning all racial protest in Danville.)

In jail I had what everybody in jail has, lots of time to think about the past, to analyze the present, and to pro-

ject about the future. Only about Judge Michie could I
think, for he was the beginning and ending of my world and
I was hopeful.

There was hope because the injunctions, statutes, and
city ordinances we had challenged were patently void. And
then the second day of jail came with its sensitizing of my
body to sounds: sounds of the phone ringing, the rattle of
the keys, the snap of the three locks between me and the
outside which consisted of the office of Harvey and Wood,
Oliver's Cafe and the singing of the mass meetings on the
hill at High Street Baptist Church—"We Shall Overcome,"
"The Demonstrating G.I. from Fort Bragg."

The hope remained even though a certain loneliness
grew as my nose gradually became imprisoned by the stench
of the nearby commode, the harsh scent of pine disinfectant,
and the aroma of well-cooked stew from the kitchen below.
Because I had insisted on not being bonded out before
those who had been in jail longer than I, I found myself
losing my world as the others would hear their names called:
"Dan Foss, git your clothes and things and come on." "Ivanhoe Donaldson, on your way."

Hope lingered even as I wondered who would come
to replace the work horses, Nat Conyers and Dean Robb
of Detroit, who had both left Danville with darkened rings
around their eyes (which gave the impression they had lost
a fight), and who had done so much to get suits filed in
federal courts, preparing legal memoranda and defending
scores of cases in the Corporation, Municipal, and Juvenile
Courts of Danville. William Kunstler and Arthur Kinoy had
left for New York to await another demand on their time.
Professor Antieu, Phil Hirschkop, Shelly Bowers, and the
others were busy in Washington, with duties that had been
abandoned for the Danville emergency. And the hope lingered regarding Judge Michie as I sat in jail.

CHAPTER 3

Choosing Sides

While confined in my world of steel, stone, and sounds I could not forget the anger of Tuesday, June 25, the day before I was jailed. Back at the High Street Church after the arguments of law with Judge Michie, an F.B.I. agent had passionately counseled against demonstrations while Judge Michie had the case under advisement. In this position he had been joined by three of the five Danville Negro lawyers. Wisely, William Kunstler, Arthur Kinoy, and some of the others had refrained from participating in the discussion of whether or not to renew demonstrations.

I opposed the participation of lawyers in this matter, feeling that keeping the lawyers out of the discussion would result in more demonstrations. Growing experience was teaching me that lawyers are conservative by nature. Having failed in keeping them out of the discussion, I made a halfhearted and brief statement to the assembled leaders in the Sunday School room of the High Street Church that I didn't think that demonstrations—one way or the other—would affect the decision. I was halfhearted in taking this position because I was also conservative . . . and not quite sure; the law on the matter seemed so obvious, and there was no way that Judge Michie could possibly find that the injunction and the anti-picketing ordinance were valid. Besides, I was tired of getting, at best, six hours' sleep and attending three different courts each day for cases and being

like a cat in a dog pound in court. Human bodies have limits.
For a while I enjoyed the forced rest in jail, the regularity of meals, good meals rather than hot dogs on the run as on the outside, and the absence of weighted decisions which could determine serious facets of hundreds of lives: "Should I continue in the Movement even though it may have serious effects on the health of my grandmother?"; "How may I get excused from court appearances on the days that final exams are scheduled in summer school?"; "Would it be all right to plead guilty and get free of punishment for all charges, as my bondsman is trying to force me to do because he's worried about the amount of money he is now obligated for?"; "Is it o.k. to go to a relative's funeral in Richmond on Tuesday?"; "How do I get the rent paid now that the City had me cut off compensation since my arrest?"

But on Friday, June 28, 1963, as Daniel Foss, Ivanhoe Donaldson, and all the others were leaving, I thought I had had enough rest, at least of that kind and in that place. Fright overcame me to some degree as I learned that I was trapped; I couldn't get out. The Movement had run out of people with property who could go bonds . . . and Martin Luther King's Southern Christian Leadership Conference wasn't sending money into Danville "because they were broke." Methodically I kept talking to myself: "Be cool, Len. Be calm, Len—be collected. Something will happen to get you out of this solitary confinement created by the others being bonded out. Something will happen, dammit!" There was bewilderment over the reason given for my having been forced to remain, alone, because all the others were gone. How could King's outfit be broke when every week *Jet* magazine was showing pictures of him getting checks for $75,000 from mammoth rallies which eventually fattened the coffers of SCLC to over $800,000 for 1963?

I was about to panic.

After playing cards and dominoes through the bars with the two colored trusties for three hours, I was calm. I had resigned myself to spending the weekend and a great deal more time, alone, in my private section of the Danville jail. I had convinced myself that there was no world beyond the barred gate at the end of the tier which led to the steps which either took you downstairs to the mess hall or upstairs to the bunks. To think about the outside was painful; therefore, it could no longer exist. It did not exist.

I ate dinner alone June 28, 1963, at the table for colored a few hours later . . . and didn't mind it. After dinner I went upstairs and had started on a proof copy of *Blues People* by LeRoi Jones. The conquest was complete. I had surrendered to the limitations of my world, its tastes, its stale and disinfectant smells; its controlling sounds of locks popping, piercing phone rings, keys jangling and the hollering clang of the front door bell.

After 6:00 P.M., when an insistent clang of the doorbell rang through the echoing chambers of the jail, I hardly noticed it. Upon hearing my name called—"Holt, you got guests," I didn't respond at first, thinking that it must be a trick of vengeance that the jailers had concocted to play to obtain their own special satisfaction.

"Snake Doctor! Baby, it's me." I heard and recognized what I thought to be the distinct Irish brogue of an old friend. I moved toward the locked door at the end of my tier in disbelief—how I could have become "stir crazy" in such a short period? It couldn't be that friend; it couldn't be Michael Standard, Bill Standard's son; Mike was in New York.

It was Mike.

Standing there as big and as beautiful as an angel with a grin so large it seemed to swallow his head, was Michael Standard—intellectual, lawyer and lovable human. And he was an angel. In his hands were papers commanding the City Sergeant to release the body of one Len Holt. I had been bonded! I was free of the world of urine and disinfectant, of well balanced and regular meals, of the sounds of clanging doorbells, rattling keys and popping locks—of loneliness.

As Mike and I hurried to O. C. Thaxton's home sixty miles away in Lynchburg, Va., in my dusty Renault that had sat parked and neglected for days, Mike explained how he had happened to come. "At the meeting of the Program and Activities Committee of the National Lawyers Guild on Thursday, word was received that you had insisted that others be bonded out before you, that the local people able to put up bond had run out, and that you would be in jail, alone. Rumors had also been picked up that you would have an 'accident' over the weekend."

Quickly the meeting had been disbanded as various members began searching for ways to raise the $5,000 bond needed in a hurry. And they had done it. Michael Standard—who had been in Danville months earlier as my co-counsel in sit-in cases involving the leaders of the Danville Movement—was given the task of taking the money to Danville and "delivering my body."

Demonstrations had temporarily ended in Danville on June 28, 1963. Hope of a favorable decision from Judge Michie of the federal court had been the major reason for this decision; it was thought to be impossible that he could rule otherwise, and some plans had been made for a victory celebration.

Then it happened. The SCLC announced on Saturday,

June 29, that a state-wide rally was being held in Danville on July 3, the coming Wednesday, that the rally would be addressed by Martin Luther King, and that groups from all over the state were being asked to converge on Danville and protest the brutality and the trials.

John Carter, the City Councilman who was a symbol of the *violent whites* of the City, and who knew that the way to contain the Negro protest for integration and jobs was to give nothing, met with James A. H. Ferguson, the City Attorney, and one or two others and mapped out a strategy that was cunningly effective.

The Vice-Mayor of Danville, George Anderson, who was the titular head of the community while Mayor Julian R. Stinson was out of the city on "business," announced: "I am confident that the local Danville Police supplemented by a contingent of State Troopers will be able to cope with any of the problems arising from the rally." On the same day, Saturday, June 30, the Reverend L. W. Chase responded: "I've received word that Dr. King will arrive here around 2:00 P.M. for an afternoon rally on July 3." The die was cast.

The Negroes of Danville were jubilant. "Dr. King will show them where it's at." "Betcha they'll talk a different tune when he comes." "I knew it! I knew it! I knew Dr. King would come and lead us so that the white folks would be sorry for all they've done." "Danville is going to have to stop messing around; they'll have to integrate or close down the city. What Dr. King did in Birmingham will look like a picnic to what he'll do here," were typical comments.

But there were some who were not so jubilant, the ten SNCC field secretaries and two CORE field secretaries. Clandestinely they tried to think of ways to get King *really* involved, to demonstrate and be arrested and to be charged with all crimes that everyone else was charged with: the felony of inciting colored people to commit acts of violence and war against the white people, disorderly conduct, resisting arrest (because he went limp when arrested), contributing to the delinquency of a minor (by having a minor in the group demonstrating when King is arrested), violating the parade ordinance, and disorderly conduct. For some reason—based partially on past experiences with Dr. King— they believed that unless King got involved in demonstrations, Danville would only be a stopping place for him to make an occasional speech.

At a rally in Suffolk, Virginia, on June 29 the local press quoted Dr. King as saying: "I plan to be an involved participant in the Danville struggle." Apparently the concern of the SNCC and CORE field secretaries was unnecessary.

On July 1 a three-judge Federal District Court sitting in Alexandria, Va., declared the state segregated-seat law unconstitutional and the Reverend Chase announced that the King rally would be held in the Negro-owned Peter's Park, where exhibition baseball games were usually held, and that a parade permit would be sought from the City to allow for the marching from the High Street Baptist Church to the site of the rally. Meanwhile, there were still no demonstrations.

Then a new twist occurred. The Movement lawyers had been taking the 300-mile round drive to Charlottesville, where Judge Michie lived and maintained an office, seeking temporary restraining orders which were never granted but always postponed for a full-scale hearing at some later date. John Carter and James Ferguson, the Danville city lawyers, decided to take the same trip; they were seeking a federal injunction against the Movement, Dr. Martin Luther King, SCLC, the Movement leaders, CORE, The Student

Nonviolent Coordinating Committee (SNCC) and me. I laughed when I heard about this move. "It's ridiculous. It's the same thing that was tried and failed in Albany, Ga., by another federal judge appointed by President Kennedy," I told those who asked what I thought of the move. "It's a move that can't hold up on appeal and is employed only when you have a federal judge that thinks he ought to use the federal power to help a community to remain segregated. With all of his Virginia upbringing, Michie is not that kind of federal judge. He'll laugh John Carter and Ferguson out of his chambers on this matter," I proclaimed.

Meanwhile the City of Danville denied the parade permit and condemned Peter's Park as being unfit for the holding of the rally.

On July 2 it came—for me the biggest surprise of modern American legal history—the Justice Department of the United States Government filed an *amicus* brief in the United States District Court for the Western District of Virginia, setting forth specifically that the United States Government thought Judge Michie should keep the cases in the federal court that we had removed to the federal court from the Danville Corporation Court, presided over by Judge Archibald M. Aiken, because it was impossible for the Negro demonstrators against segregation in Danville to receive a fair trial before Judge Aiken, the only judge in Danville before whom the cases could be tried.

"Whoopee!" I shouted in the corridor of City Hall when Jerry Williams, in a voice of forced calmness, showed me the copy of the *amicus* petition of the United States Government that he had received in his morning mail.

It was 2:00 P.M. It was a moment of triumph.

It was a moment of fulfillment of the efforts of William M. Kunstler who had pushed the action of removing state criminal cases in the south to federal courts when it was clear that those protesting against segregation could not get fair trials in a state court that was as much a part of the pattern of racism as the segregated toilets present in the state courtroom. Every civil rights legal group, such as the NAACP Legal Defense & Educational Fund, and every civil rights lawyer, including me, had heretofore expressed doubt about the wisdom of the move or outrightly opposed it as a legal tactic. At 2:00 P.M. on July 2, in Danville and all over the south, it was the day of William M. Kunstler. So exuberant was I that I kissed Jerry Williams on the cheek—only to learn why the ladies want their men to shave. I was stuck by an outgrowth of beard resulting from the sixteen to eighteen hours a day schedule that Jerry Williams and all of us had been following.

It was 2:00 P.M., Tuesday, July 2, 1963 and I was happy. And I needed this good news because only hours earlier in the Municipal Court of Danville Larry Wilson, the assistant Commonwealth Attorney of Danville, had physically leaped upon me, knocked me down, and snatched a warrant from my hand as I was defending some demonstrators. It was good news and needed news at 2:00 P.M.

And the hour was a time of sober thinking and some embarrassment.

I had treated Alan Marer of the Justice Department with unconcealed disdain. Disdain born of being involved in, or knowing about, thousands of reports and instances where either the Justice Department or the F.B.I. had taken affidavits or made investigations of violations of civil rights of Negroes and done nothing, even though the violations of Negro rights were absolutely clear. Nothing, but nothing, had been done: Tallahassee, Atlanta, Birmingham, Gadsden, Moulton, Louisville, Monroe, Jackson, McComb, Greenwood, Lynchburg, Petersburg, Hopewell, Montgomery, Nashville, and other places—nothing had been done with the countless reports.

In the *amicus* brief of the United States Government was the unmistakable hand of Alan Marer—who had been subjected to so much scorn.

As Jerry Williams and I rejoiced, as only two happy Negroes can in the midst of angry whites in a City Hall, I was tempted to forget the politics that the Kennedy boys had played with Governor Patterson of Alabama during the Freedom Rides of 1961 two years before, which nearly resulted in the death of those whom I had advised to take the bus on to Montgomery "because I've been assured that the bus will get through by Wyatt Walker of SCLC, who is in personal contact with the Attorney General." For a moment during the rejoicing in the corridor of the Danville City Hall I had forgotten that the bus carrying the Freedom Riders did "get through" but the Freedom Riders narrowly escaped death in an orgy of violence encouraged by the absence of police protection at the bus terminal in Montgomery when the bus did arrive. We were tempted to forget until Mrs. Mary Shirley Thomas came up and asked us a question about where the Movement mass meeting was going to be that night.

Across her face was an ugly gouging scar. It was her burden for having defiantly pursued an ephemeral concept called Freedom. That scar across her face was her lifetime reminder of the beating she had suffered—along with forty-six others on the night of June 10, 1963, in Danville at the hands of Danville's "finest."

Our rejoicing stopped. Jerry Williams and I were plunged back into reality. In stumbling fashion we managed to tell Mrs. Thomas we didn't know where the mass meet-

ing was. It was 2:09 P.M. and Jerry and I weren't as happy as
we had been moments before.

Mrs. Thomas' scarred face had reminded us that whatever had been received from Washington and the Justice
Department had come at the price of her disfigurement,
the brutalizing of forty-six others and the denial of basic
rights to twelve thousand other black Danville citizens. She
had reminded us that the world had recoiled in shock at
the gory pictures and news of what happened and that the
Justice Department had to act—lest it seem to be aligned
with the forces that had inflicted the beatings in Danville
in the name of "law and order." It was then that we realized
that what the Justice Department had done was little indeed.

And it was.

Yet, this was quite a day July 2, 1963. At last the Justice
Department of the United States had lined up in favor
of the civil rights viewpoint that justice for integrationists is
an "accident" in southern courts. Section 1443 of Title 28 of
the United States Code had come to life again after being
dead for nearly one hundred years since its passage as part of
the Reconstruction legislation.

This was to be more of a day. As a result of Danville
the right of Negroes was established to appeal the remand
of cases to a state court by a federal judge. Appeals of the
remand could go to the United States Courts of Appeals
and then to the United States Supreme Court. These rights
were later incorporated into the Civil Rights Bill of 1964.
Prior to Danville and the push given to the removal statutes
invoked there, a Negro who had removed his case from the
state court had no right of appeal if a federal judge sent the
cases back to the state court from which they had been removed.

It was 3:00 P.M. before I was able to leave the Danville City Hall for that day. I still felt good. Movement lawyers were in Charlottesville on the matter of the silly federal injunction that John W. Carter and Ferguson were seeking in order to enjoin protest . . . and the July 3 meeting where King had promised to come and speak and to lead the folks of Danville as he had led the people of Birmingham only two months earlier in May.

Conceive of a mother putting strychnine in her baby's milk. Try to imagine the feeling that Caesar had when Brutus plunged the dagger into his chest. Place yourself within the feeling of Jesus when Judas gave him the betraying kiss or the Apostle Peter denied him thrice. Then add some more of the same. Even with all that you will not be able to understand fully the depth of disappointment that rolled like a wave of human excrement being spewed forth from a volcano-like septic tank throughout the Danville Negro community shortly after 5:00 P.M. on the day of "triumph," July 2, 1963.

Judge Michie, the United States Federal District Judge for the Western District of Virginia, at 5:00 P.M. signed a sweeping injunction giving John W. Carter and the other powers of Danville everything they had asked for; the federal judge had—in the name of protecting the people represented by John W. Carter (certain elements of the white community because Carter's views did not correspond with those of the Negroes seeking integration) enjoined the movement. Judge Michie had accepted the viewpoint of Chief McCain, John W. Carter, Mayor Stinson and the others.

His order went even further than that of Judge Aiken in some respects. The laws of Danville were racist laws designed for the sole purpose of maintaining segregation and

the segregationist who passed them, yet the federal court
in part of its order said all were enjoined

>   . . . from participating in, financing, sponsoring, encour-
>   aging or engaging in meetings or other activities whereby the
>   violation of the laws of the Commonwealth of Virginia, City of
>   Danville, or the terms of this restraining order are suggested,
>   advocated or encouraged.

Named as persons enjoined by his restraining order were

Lawrence George Campbell, Alexander I. Dunlap, L. W. Chase,
Danville Progressive Christian Association, an unincorporated
association; Milton A. Reid, Virginia Christian Leadership Conference, an unincorporated association; Martin Luther King Jr.,
Southern Christian Leadership Conference, an unincorporated
association; John Robert Zellner, James Forman, Student Non-
Violent Coordinating Committee (SNCC), an unincorporated
association; Len Holt, Congress of Racial Equality, a New York
Corporation; and all persons conspiring or acting in concert
with them, be and they are hereby restrained from conspiring
to deny the citizens of Danville, Virginia, equal protection, privilege and immunities under the laws of the Commonwealth of
Virginia and the City of Danville.

The day provided another disappointment. The Movement leaders called the Reverend Martin Luther King in
Atlanta and informed him of the events of the day—especially the federal injunction—and were greeted with this
announcement: "Tell the people that I shall, regrettably, not
be able to come to Danville at this time because of pressing
business involving SCLC in Atlanta."
Few attended the mass meeting that night, word about

developments having reached most people via television and radio long before time for going to the church.

Down at the office of Harvey and Wood—headquarters for the legal effort in defense of the Movement—nobody said much. Sensing that, in spite of my prior experiences with federal judges and with Judge Michie, I took it hardest, Harry Wood said little.

After dinner, which consisted of hog maws, blackeyed peas, cabbage, cornbread, and beer at Oliver's Cafe on Spring Street, Harry Wood, "Lawyer Mac," and I hardly talked to each other. The people crowded in there eating and talking and drinking beer somehow sensed we were in the dumps and refrained from their usual questions about what had happened that day in court or why it had happened.

The white Renault wound its way back up South Main Street to the office. "Mac," Harry, and I disembarked. Once getting in the office, Harry handed me a medium-sized bag, saying: "Here's a present for you. I've been saving it for a day like this when you might need it." Instinctively I said, "Thanks."

As I began to open the package Harry kept talking. "We've done one helluva job here. The people appreciate it." Raising his voice and becoming impassionate, Harry nearly shouted as the tears filled his eyes: "Damn the bastards! Damn them!"

Because Harry was expressing our own emotions, the moment seemed sacred, and since we didn't know how to say it any better we contributed to the liturgy with silence. It was nearly 7:00 P.M.

In the bag was a fifth of Gordon's gin and a big hunk of cheese. Harry and "Mac," the secretary whom we called "Lawyer Mac," were teetotalers and withdrew into the other offices. I began the search for escape in consecutive glasses of straight gin. I started to read for the first time the language of the *amicus* brief the United States Government filed that morning which had caused our rejoicing before we heard the news about Judge Michie and the federal court. The *amicus* brief of the Justice Department— a partial payment for a night of infamy and a lifetime of degradation of Danville Negroes—read well and almost seemed poetic as the glasses of gin moved me deeper and deeper in the world of "I don't care":

The evidence adduced at the hearing in Danville on June 24-25, 1963, reveals, *inter alia*, that Judge Aiken, who will hear all of the pending contempt charges, was himself involved in attempting to disperse crowds of demonstrators at an earlier date. He also testified that he feared that trouble or violence of one kind or another might occur as a result of the demonstrations; indeed, at one point in his testimony he said that he considered that certain types of demonstrations which he had observed amounted to "violence," and were "sinister" and "menacing," although no actual physical violence occurred. *In view of this evidence, it is difficult to believe that petitioners will be able to obtain a fair trial before Judge Aiken* [italics mine]. And if they cannot do so, whatever defense they may wish to assert grounded upon their right to demonstrate for the purpose of obtaining the equal protection of the laws *may well go for nought in Judge Aiken's court* [italics mine]. If that is true, then, we submit, petitioners should be classified as persons who are "denied or cannot enforce in the courts of (the) State a right under any law providing for equal civil rights . . ."

Indeed, there is much more involved here than the mere denial of a fair trial. The trial itself is being conducted in a most unjudicial atmosphere. The Judge conceded that he has been armed with a pistol which he removes only when reaching his office. One witness testified in fact that Judge Aiken was armed on the bench. However that may be, the fact remains that it is common knowledge that the trial Judge is armed, and this alone is bound to intimidate Negro citizens of Danville, to reduce their expectations of obtaining a fair trial in the Corporation Court, and thus to interfere with their campaign for equal civil rights. Moreover, the evidence reveals that Negro counsel, male and female, have been searched upon entering the courtroom; that the courtroom has been closed to the public (except to the press); that perhaps 40-odd armed police officers were stationed throughout the courtroom during the two contempt trials which have already taken place; *that the Judge had prepared, in advance of trial, a written memorandum of his decision finding the first two defendants guilty of contempt* [italics mine]; and that Judge Aiken refused to examine into the contention made upon motion of the defendants just prior to the first trial, that the Corporation Court had no jurisdiction to proceed because, as this Court subsequently held on June 25, 1963, filing of the removal petitions transferred the cases to this Court and ousted the Corporation Court of any power to act upon them. This conduct of Judge Aiken surely suggests that he will be somewhat unreceptive to arguments grounded upon controlling federal law. *Furthermore, Judge Aiken refused to release on bail, pending appeal, the two defendants convicted of contempt* [italics mine]. Since the sentences imposed are relatively short, this ruling—which Judge Aiken apparently intends to apply to all the pending contempt cases—effectively denies appellate review of his judgments of guilt. And, finally, the practice of imposing 45 and 60-day jail terms in contested cases, while imposing either no confinement as in one case, or only a two-day term, as in the second case, upon the two defendants who pleaded guilty, simply exacerbates the situation by suggesting that those who choose to assert their rights will suffer the consequences.

The combination of a trier of fact who has apparently prejudged the issues and was a participant in the events culminating in the very charges to be tried, considered together with the general atmosphere of the proceedings and its inevitable results, makes *it quite clear, it seems to us, that a fair trial cannot be had in the Corporation Court* [italics mine].

Harry Wood read the same document and posed a succinct question: "How did all this start . . . and why in Danville? On the surface it seems like a nice small town in the Midwest or anywhere. It has clean streets and bustling businesses—at least before the Negro boycott—and all its ugliness is hidden in well-concealed slums far from the paths of visitors, just like 100,000 other communities in America. Give, baby, how did the ugliness get out in the open?"

I didn't answer Harry, at least not aloud so that he could hear it and I only partially answered the questions to myself, simply because there were only parts of the answer known to me. "How does the bestiality of a community suddenly express itself in its crudest forms after being submerged for so long?

Why and how Danville? Let us go back to 1960.

CHAPTER 4

The Myths

> *Justice and peace are complimen-*
> *tary terms; they can only exist to-*
> *gether. This is why the* white man's
> peace *is for us a* slave's peace. *We*
> *can never again accept or keep such*
> *a peace.*
> —Mike Thelwell, *Bitterness*

Several years ago Harry Golden, in full jest, suggested that the racial strife in the South could be reduced if his "Golden Plan" were adopted. He outlined how chaos was caused when white folks thought they were going to be sitting with Negroes and that therefore chairs should be removed from all public places allowing for integration—verti-cal integration.

Harry Golden in his *Carolina Israelite* was joking.

Danville wasn't.

In 1960 after a successful suit was brought by Jerry Williams, Andrew Muse, Harry Wood, and Miss Ruth Har-vey on behalf of their clients to integrate the Danville Library, now a Confederate Memorial but once the last capitol of the confederacy, the library was closed.

Again John W. Carter was fighting on the wrong side—at least as most Americans claim to view rightness these days. His impassioned pleas to preserve the sanctity of the last capitol of the Confederacy for whites only having failed, officials of the city projected a novel plan—take out of the Library all of the seats.

Harry Golden's humor became Danville's reality. It became the first place in the South to implement an asinine joke. That is the Danville of 1960 and, unhappily, that is the Danville of today.

Danville is 60 miles south of an aptly named town in Virginia called Lynchburg (the place where the word "lynch law" was introduced into the English language) down U.S. Route 29 where that highway intersects U.S. Route 58. It's 45 miles north of Greensboro, North Carolina. To the west of Danville some 30 miles is the infamous town of Martinsville, Virginia, whose notoriety stems from the electrocution of seven Negroes accused of rape by one white woman.

One could say that Danville is a town located on the Dan River consisting of homes and office buildings splattered out from the nearly ten or so factories of the Dan River Mills, whose power in the town is reflected by the fact that it employs 10,000 persons and Danville has a population of only 47,000.

At a wide bend in the Dan River, this city, which is typical of the "New South," is one of Virginia's purely industrial communities with tobacco as the backbone of income in its shipping and trading and where cotton manufacturing is "King."

And the King's name is Dan River Mills.

Yet Danville is attached, somewhat reluctantly, to the world—seven main highways converge into its Main Street.

The visitor coming into town on North Main comes through a cramped area of cotton mills and pungent, cavernous tobacco warehouses, redrying, and storage plants, then reaches a business section where neon signs make little rain-

bows at night, and sees a 12-story Masonic Temple that is a
few yards away from an opulent-looking City Hall of conventional classic design which conceals much of the ancient
jail separated from the City Hall by a small, and much too
convenient, alley.

Passing through the business district and onto West
Main one goes toward impressive homes of another day
vainly clinging to their glory as commercial usages infiltrate.
A little beyond one finds Averette Junior College, which is
mostly a finishing school for well-to-do girls. And on just a
little farther one will find such pretentious names as Lady
Astor Street, named for a local girl "who made it" and became a member of the British Parliament.

At one time the city had a slogan: "Danville Does
Things." Such a boast could rest on the solid achievement of
about 769,000 spindles and 17,000 looms . . . and the fact
that the city is the "World's Best Tobacco Market."

Being at the heart of the "old belt" of bright tobacco
growing, the city gathers for the world market the flue-cured
leaf which is the base of tobacco blends and the mainstay of
the world's cigarette industry. In the late summer and for a
couple of months thereafter, during the short season of marketing, its vast auction warehouses resound with the sing-
song, twangy jargons of auctioneers and buyers.

As a tobacco marketing town, Danville's career began
in 1793 when the coarse and sincere Piedmont planters, irked
by the hardship of rolling hogsheads over a hundred miles
of red clay roads to Richmond for the inspection, got the
legislature to set up an inspection station at this broad point
of the Dan River.

Danville's industrial era started in 1881 with the opening
of a small yarn mill and with the harnessing of power from

the river and the influx of cheap labor from the farms and mountain settlements.

Danville is America. It's New York City, Sioux City, Pomona, Helena, San Diego, Spokane; it's everywhere one can find a group of *kikes, wops, sheenies, dagoes, polacks, coons, spics, bohunks,* who live in ghettos they can't escape, and who must of necessity suffer a thousand-times-a-thousand daily reminders, of both an overt and covert nature, which whisper or scream, "stay in your place, the one I've made for you."

Danville is anywhere in America where the city fathers believe "their" Negroes are content.

Danville is anywhere Negroes are convinced that the local police force won't break open their heads or shoot them down in the name of "law and order" for engaging in peaceful protest and then be able to justify the murders to the larger community population with magic words like "communist," "hoodlum," "outsider."

Both fictions were in active employment in Danville. I can recall the comment of the Reverend A. I. Dunlap in Lynchburg in the spring of 1962 when he was there observing the trial of one facet of the *Lynchburg Omnibus Integration Suit.* "Man, they don't want any trouble in Danville. If we ask them to integrate something and show that it's a serious concern, they'll do it. They don't want any trouble. During the lunch counter sit-ins of 1960 they wouldn't even arrest anyone."

This was amazing. My partners, Joe Jordan and Ed Dawley, and I had worked harder in 1960 than in many a year defending those arrested for lunch counter sit-ins in Virginia cities considered far more liberal than Danville: cities such as Norfolk, Newport News, and Richmond.

And the larger white community thought all was well in Danville with its Negroes. The only integration suit brought in a long time was to integrate the Danville Library and this was quickly resolved by the "vertical integration plan." No suits had been brought to integrate schools. Not a "peep" of dissent had been raised about the segregated recreational system, public housing, toilets, and drinking fountains in public buildings, nor about the racially segregated cemeteries and hospitals.

Further confirmation was provided for Dunlap's view when the *Danville Omnibus Integration Suit* was filed in federal court in the summer of 1962. Dunlap and other Movement leaders were the plaintiffs in this suit; I was their lawyer. Even before the matter came to trial the signs above toilets and drinking fountains were yanked down. Courtroom segregation was ended for anyone bold enough to challenge it while waiting to be tried before a judge who could notice that the usual practice of racial seating was not being adhered to. And black and handsome Julius Adams got a bit of integration he doesn't want to use: a burial plot in the previously all-white city cemetery. Down went the racial barriers in the city recreation system to those who applied— as the city stopped sponsoring public dances for teen-agers. In line fell the City Armory which was used as a place for large public gatherings, and which prior to the filing of the *Omnibus Integration Suit* was barred to use by Negroes. In a most befitting way the Danville Movement asserted itself in the Armory.

In March of 1963 the Danville Branch of SCLC sponsored a meeting with Dr. Martin Luther King as the featured speaker. As per expectation, his speech was rousing and satisfying to the burning souls of 2,500 Danville Negroes who packed every available seat and space allowed by the extremely *vigilant* fire and police department.

"And justice will flow over Danville like a stream from a mighty water," Dr. King exhorted. Pride, determination, and suppressed desires all welled forth in black bosoms as the crowd spoke back to King with "Yeah's," "Tell it!" "My Lord!" Preceding Dr. King and in somber contrast because of the blunt terseness of his message was a stocky, determined Irishman with black horn-rimmed glasses and silver-haired crewcut missing all but the faintest suggestion of once having been a rich black: Carl Braden.

"I'm an integrationist, a field secretary for the Southern Conference Educational Fund (SCEF). I stand here ready to do whatever may be needed to support the Movement and our local board member Alexander Dunlap. I'll go to jail again for what I believe: that segregation is wrong." With his chin jutting forth and tones so firm, no one doubted Carl Braden meant every word of his remarks made in the three minutes he spoke. Onward went the mass meeting. Onward went the hope that Danville would become an "open city" if the Negroes merely convinced the *City Hall* that the integrated community was really desired beyond the level of mere discussion.

And there was nothing on the horizon in March or April or May of 1963 in Danville, the home of Dan River Fabrics and Dan River Mills, to suggest that full integration wouldn't come if there were meaningful protest—except the "minority voice" of John W. Carter on the city council.

I made no plans for the hot, hellish summer in the damnation of Danville, nor did Lawrence G. Campbell, Alexander I. Dunlap, Lendell W. Chase or Julius Adams, the Movement leaders. Back in my Norfolk, Va., home, I made

inquiry about how to get a passport and how to spend the
summer and the rest of the year abroad. Finding no way to
finance such a trip, I would spend the summer on Fire Island
or with friends in San Francisco. I was tired, tired of so
many things in so many ways: tired of long drives, alone,
down country roads in Georgia, Virginia, Alabama, North
Carolina—and even Mississippi, if the phone calls came
asking for the "Snake Doctor." I wanted rest from being like
a balloon in a pin factory as judge after judge threatened me
with contempt for suggesting such things as courtroom desegregation or for raising legal points that found disfavor. I was
tired of being subpoenaed down to the Norfolk city treasurer's office two or three times a year to explain why I hadn't
listed on my state income tax form income from CORE
(which I had not worked for in three years) and tired of
being called before the local representative of the Internal
Revenue Service in Norfolk who had decided that in his own
way he would stop me from attacking the things sacred to
a segregated life—and feeling quite embarrassed when at
one conference a group of clippings fell on the floor from the
official file which showed me handling integration cases in
different parts of Virginia, Georgia, and Alabama. The citing
of Ed Dawley, my partner, and myself by Judge Holiday in
the Circuit Court of Hopewell, Va., and failure for the first
time to get a contempt charge dismissed without appealing,
also bore heavy.*

After two short trips to Birmingham in the midst of the
racial protest there in May of 1963 and observing James
Forman give a hand to the Reverend Fred Shuttlesworth in
planning demonstrations there, I needed a rest. Dr. Cejas
had warned me that failure to rest more would mean putting

*On January 18, 1965, the United States Supreme Court agreed to hear
our appeal (granted *certiorari*).

me back on maalox. I was just plain ol' fashioned tired, so tired I could have slept a year.

The same situation was present with the leaders of the Danville Movement. The Reverend Alexander Dunlap, "Lap," was packing his bags and heading for Kittrell College as the Vice-President. The Reverend Lawrence G. Campbell was planning the expansion of the church, the Bibleway Holiness Church, in both its social service program and physical facilities, as he continued to sell insurance for the Southern Aid Life Insurance Company of Virginia and told the story of Negro Danville on the weekly radio broadcasts originating from the Bibleway Church.

But the summer did come, and the plans, as well made as they were, all changed because neither the white community of Danville nor the black community had correctly assessed each other's fictions.

CHAPTER 5

Genesis

Wisdom is no virtue
During the times of impatient men.

For knowledge makes one a fool
and stands in the way of the miracle
of a people who are being pushed off a cliff
and who fall—upward.
— "The Wisdom of Dawley"

A mighty black surge swept forth among the Negroes of America in 1960 without serving notice of its coming. It was dominated by the concepts of Christianity and came like the return predicted for Christ: "A thief by day, a robber by night." The sedentary name "sit-in" belied its nature, actively disruptive both to white America and the institutions of black America.

The school administrations of Negro colleges had convinced themselves that the highest, and only, ambition of thousands of students in segregated colleges in the South was to get a union card, called a "degree," and go forth in their communities seeking the sickening existence of the *Black Bourgeoisie,* written about so well by E. Franklin Frazier, which is characterized by the pursuit of creature comforts: cars, houses, parties, and the quest for bridge prizes.

The spark was Greensboro, N.C., and the four students

from A&T State College who sat at a Woolworth lunch counter on February 1. The rest is history.

Also caught unprepared was the National Association for the Advancement of Colored People (NAACP). For years this organization had waged a persistent—although slow and piecemeal—war against forms of racial segregation in America. Its approach was primarily that of preparing and filing cases which secured federal court orders forbidding some state officials from practicing segregation.

The other activities of the NAACP, such as lobbying for the passage of legislation on lynching and voting, met with less success, and tended to be forgotten when Negroes discussed the organization. Its stature grew and grew, so much so that people in the Negro communities sometimes listed membership in the NAACP as one might list an honorary college degree, and battles for the presidency of twenty and thirty-member chapters sometimes assumed gigantic proportions. The NAACP was the "alpha and omega" of civil rights. Rightly or wrongly, every Negro fortunate enough to be exposed to knowledge about the NAACP's work considered it to be the place that any Negro could turn whenever a wrong was inflicted. It was the fiber of the being of Negro rights and the struggle for those rights . . . until 1960.

The Congress of Racial Equality (CORE), the New York-based civil rights organization founded in 1947, which emphasized direct action and nonviolence in protesting against racial segregation, had but two field secretaries and a budget of less than $50,000 before the 1960 sit-ins. Its budget now approaches a million dollars and it has an estimated thirty-five field secretaries.

In 1960 when the sit-ins began, the Student Nonviolent Coordinating Committee (SNCC) was not in existence. Now

SNCC is the civil rights organization with the largest staff, more than 250 persons, mostly concentrated in Mississippi— and a budget in excess of $1,000,000.

With no field staff in 1960 and a budget of less than $60,000, Dr. Martin Luther King's SCLC has expanded to a field staff of a little less than thirty persons and a budget approaching a million dollars.

This information is important when one considers that there is nothing about the nature or program of the three other major civil rights organizations (SNCC, CORE, and SCLC) which is not encompassable within the framework of the NAACP.

Nothing except "wisdom" and unwillingness.

Strangely enough, many of the local chapters of the NAACP throughout the country, and especially the south, reflected, and possibly initiated, the hesitancy of getting involved in any but the most token racial protest. In town after town, the leaders of the local NAACP chapters were considered the "Respectable and Responsible" Negroes and were the ones with whom the white power structure of communities conducted dialogues.

Danville, Va., was no exception.

Greensboro, N.C., where the sit-in movement of the 1960's began, is but 43 miles to the south of Danville; its newspapers are widely read in Danville. Its capacity for stirring protests was deeply felt in Danville.

But a far more pronounced influence was exerted in Danville by the concept and image of Dr. Martin Luther King, president and founder of SCLC. A measure of this influence can be understood, partly, if one realizes that there is hardly a Negro alive who has heard of, or seen, Dr. King who has not expressed deep admiration, if not deification, of him. Especially is this so of the ministers of the South.

King's projection as *the* civil rights leader raised the whole level of self-esteem of the Negro preachers in the South. Wisely, King assessed this esteem and identification and made the basis of his organization the anxious-to-identify preacher. His appeal to the Southern clergy was so great that counter-organizational efforts of various NAACP officials among some of their staunchest ministerial supporters were in vain.

By reason of impatience, because of the inspiration of nearby Greensboro and because of disgust with the "conservative" leadership of the Reverend Doyle Thomas of the Loyal Baptist Church of Danville—and other minor reasons —the Reverend Lawrence G. Campbell, Julius Adams, and the Reverend Alexander I. Dunlap activated a branch of the Southern Christian Leadership Conference in Danville, the Danville SCLC.

The move infuriated Reverend Thomas and other leaders of the Danville branch of the NAACP.

With great frequency Campbell, Dunlap, Adams, and the Reverend Lendell W. Chase (who was made president of the SCLC chapter and who was pastor of the "status" Baptist church in the Danville Negro community, High Street), began appearing before the Danville City Council in 1962. They would demand representation of Negroes on various boards running city agencies, school integration, desegregation of the facilities of City Hall, including the courtrooms, and better recreational facilities for the Negro community along with integration of eating facilities throughout the City.

As the word got around about the appearances before City Council, the leaders of the SCLC chapter achieved a new status in the Community and became "those boys with guts." On the Sunday morning broadcast from the Bibleway

Holiness Church, on radio station WILA, the Reverend
Campbell would further spread the word of confrontation
with City Hall.

From polite brush-offs the City Council switched to the
hostile honesty of John W. Carter, one of the councilmen, in
discouraging further petitions from the SCLC.

Reverend Doyle Thomas questioned the motivation in
such petitioning. In their pulpits and elsewhere, the leadership of the Danville SCLC questioned more than Thomas'
motivation; they questioned him.

Aside from the disquieting reaction of elements of the
white Danville power structure that all the talk about integration wasn't good ("Somebody might start believing
it,") nothing was done except to take steps to cut off the
meetings of the City Council as a forum for the integration
ideas.

In August of 1962 things took an uneasy turn.

Massive marches under the leadership of Dr. Martin
Luther King were in full force in Albany, Ga. To all ministers in the SCLC Dr. King sent a call for help in Albany;
volunteers were to come down to fill the jails. To this challenge to enlist one's body in aid of fulfillment of Dr. King's
promise to "tear down all the walls of segregation in Albany"
the Reverend Alexander Dunlap of Danville and Julius
Adams responded. It was on the way back from Albany that
the incident happened.

The trip to Albany had been taken in Dunlap's chalky
white, newly acquired, used 1960 Cadillac. Unhappily, the
car had a faulty generator. By what was at first considered
to be a fortunate circumstance, the car's battery began to
malfunction just as Dunlap and Adams were approaching
a Sinclair service station in a small Georgia town. After

driving into the service station Dunlap spoke to the operator:

"Hi there. Got a little trouble. Like to get a charge on my battery," Dunlap, thirty-three, spoke with a broad smile on a well-formed face free of any wrinkles of age.

"Nigger, get that car out of here," snarled the white operator whose frame was dwarfed by Dunlap's 6-foot, 3-inch, 220-pound ebony frame.

"But, I can't move it. The battery is dead," Dunlap pleaded.

"I don't give a damn! Get it out of here!" With this the white service station operator drew a gun as Dunlap and Adams went to the rear of the huge white Cadillac to push it out of the station.

As they pushed, the service station operator kicked Dunlap again and again. And the same treatment was given to Julius Adams, who is a proud and dedicated Negro mill worker at Dan River, in his forties, not as enormous as the Reverend Dunlap but just as powerful.

Man has yet to devise an instrument to measure the anger, hurt, and soreness experienced by Adams and Dunlap from that racial encounter. Jokingly a week later they spoke of the experience as "turning the other cheek" but there's a certain white man in Georgia who had best pray that he never heads north and encounters two black men who once passed through a Georgia town. But the kicking probably hurt Danville more in the long run. It spilled over, partially, and became a long distance phone call to Norfolk, Va., to the offices of Jordan, Dawley, and Holt, attorneys.

"Snake, file that *Omnibus Integration Suit*—at once!" Dunlap commanded. On a musty, hot day in August of 1962 when there was not the faintest breeze blowing, Chase, Dunlap, Adams, and Campbell signed a suit in the office of a local undertaker shortly after the noon hour. Later that day the suit was filed in the Clerk's Office of the United States District Court for the Western District of Virginia.

The shock in the white community was predictable.

The Danville *Omnibus Integration Suit* asked for the integration of practically everything: the Danville Memorial Hospital, the Danville Technical Institute, cemeteries, the City Armory, Nursing Home for the aged, public housing projects, all public buildings, teacher assignments, all city employment.

While efforts were being made by Danville's City Hall to secure lawyers in Lynchburg to defend it and to delay the inevitable, a new note of seriousness entered into Danville's racial picture. Local Danville papers began to pour on the criticism of the four plaintiffs in the suit . . . as Councilman John W. Carter began to get a better audience from his colleagues: "I told you so," he began saying.

John W. Carter is a medium-sized man of no more than 5 feet, 10 inches, with close-cut steel gray hair. If one wanted to make a recruiting poster for the Marines showing a rugged drill sergeant, Carter's profile would be perfect with its sharp, hard features accentuated by a mouth with wrinkles around it that enhance his snarls. His voice was the one that asserted: be tough, never give a colored *boy* nothing, be firm—always.

Of the same mind were Mayor Julian Stinson of Danville and the other city councilmen. If there was difference, it was over how the ideas should be expressed; let them be expressed with finesse, keeping up the good front of the tolerant and understanding Virginia gentleman.

But a new factor was to enter the Danville equation: scandal.

There isn't a police force of any size in this country

where members are not involved in some lawlessness for personal gain: in Jackson, Miss., the joints selling moonshine are forced to buy part of their supply from policemen who operate stills. On Saturday nights in Birmingham squads of policemen boldly collect payoff as if they were nothing more than insurance agents. In New York's Harlem the dope, gambling, and prostitution graft payments can, and do, exceed the patrolman's salary. Danville is no exception.

Such arrangements are open secrets. Often they are shared directly with those on all levels of city government. The only real crime in these matters is getting caught in a special manner: one in which adverse publicity results and fellow policemen are forced to "cast the first stone."

May was an eventful month in 1963: the Birmingham demonstrations were receiving national attention with the dogs, "Bull" Connor, fire hoses, clubs, and injunctions; in Greensboro, 2,000 A&T College students blocked downtown traffic on successive nights to force holdout restaurants to integrate; in Danville, Sergeant Raymond Hall of the Danville Police Department was arrested.

Raymond Hall is a broad, heavy, big-boned man who looks squatty because of his bulging stomach and pale white skin, which seems immune to sun-tanning. Hall was accused of attempting to bribe a U.S. Treasury agent to keep silent about illegal traffic in bootleg liquor.

For obscure reasons, the United States Government handed the matter over to the Danville Corporation Court, presided over by Judge Aiken. In the Corporation Court the acquittal was swift. The evidence introduced consisted of a tape recording of a conversation that is supposed to have taken place between Sergeant Hall and the agent. Judge Aiken threw out the tape as evidence and the all-white jury refused to believe the testimony of the agent, who is a Negro.

Wisely, Hall had selected John W. Carter to represent him . . . but things still got disturbed. Chief Eugene Mc-Cain bounced Hall from the police force. Carter then got involved in efforts to reinstate Hall . . . which failed.

Another scandal materialized as a city councilman accused another city official of making an illegal profit from a contract and in return was sued for libel.

Something was needed to direct the attention of the citizens away from the affairs and conduct of the officials. Something was needed that would consume interest and that could be turned into a crusade or "holy war" before more closets would be opened.

On May 31, 1963, the demonstrations began.

Events moved—swiftly.

On learning that a demonstration through the streets of Danville was planned, without a request coming from Movement leaders, the City Manager, T. E. Temple, issued a parade permit and had it rushed to the point of origin of the protest: the Spring Street Municipal parking lot where approximately fifty demonstrators had gathered, mostly high school students. Careful instructions were given to the police to avoid making any arrests: "All they want is for us to do something so they can claim some sort of fame."

City Hall believed that if Dunlap, Campbell, and Adams were left alone, after a couple of days the protesting would be forgotten in favor of more comfortable pursuits than walking around Danville in 90° temperatures. The Movement was without organization, was without support from the more substantial Negroes of the city, had no local lawyers, no nothing.

Within the Movement other presumptions were operative. The March Mass Meeting, during which the City Armory had been integrated as the Movement presented

Dr. King to an overflow crowd, had given Dunlap, Campbell, and Adams status; they could bring Dr. Martin Luther King to town. They had done it once and they could do it again. And when he came again it could be for more than mere speech making, but demonstrating as well. As the month of May drew to a close Martin Luther King's name had become a holy symbol by reason of the extensive and favorable news coverage of his efforts in Birmingham. He had set the country aflame with talk about "Freedom."

Another operative assumption was a strong faith in the masses of Negroes. The Movement leaders believed that if protests were made, the bulk of the lower income groups among Danville's 11,500 Negroes would join.

Lastly there was the operative assumption that the token demands for biracial committees, integration of facilities, and biracial membership on the planning boards and commissions would quickly come if Danville's Negroes, who constituted 25 per cent of the population, made any serious expression of concern. The spontaneous and frantic sending of an unsought parade permit was considered partial confirmation of this.

Down Spring, right on Union and then along Main Street before going to the steps of the City Hall, the demonstrators walked, marched, shouted, and sang . . . as the Reverend Doyle Thomas, head of the local NAACP and the Reverend Lendell Chase, the head of the Danville SCLC, condemned the marchers and their leaders as being "unwise" and preventative of real progress—a breakthrough on the hiring of clerks in some of the stores was supposed to be imminent.

As they marched, Dunlap's screeching tenor voice led out: "Ain't gonna let nobody turn me round," and all the other marchers picked up the refrain of the song.

"What do you want?"

"Freedom!" would be the reply.

"What do I want?"

"Freedom!"

"What does everybody want—let me hear ya say it!"

"Freedom! Freedom!!" would be the forceful chorus. The black citizens gathered around or viewing the spectacle appeared to be as amazed as they were proud. White people on the streets appeared to be wondering: "Is this the beginning of our Birmingham?"

Eventually the demonstrators marched to and settled themselves upon the thirty steps of the north entrance of City Hall—both around and in front of the sacred statue of the late Mayor Wooding. Wooding's bronze image said nothing as the demonstrators' voices rang out in such songs as "Everybody Wants Freedom" and "Let My People Go" with all the vigor that young people can pour into something they intensely feel. But white citizens did say something: "It's a disgrace."

Mayor George Wooding was a Civil War hero for the Confederates and had been mayor of Danville from 1896 until his death in 1936.

For five days the same pattern continued of forming groups on the parking lot after high school had let out, forming a column of five or more abreast, marching to the rhythm of songs and shouts about freedom—but officially the Movement didn't exist.

None of the five radio stations whose programs served the area said a word. The City's two daily papers, the Danville *Register* (morning) and the Danville *Bee* (evening), which are owned by the same company, closed their eyes.

The first mention in the press was on June 5, 1963, when the arrests of Dunlap, Campbell, and a couple of others occurred. On that day the *Bee* ran an editorial that Danville would resist protest movements because, "It has too many peaceful-minded Negroes in the upper age brackets to see that the record of racial homogeneity shall not be broken down, even if lawless elements are fortified by the *federal courts* and the *Kennedy Administration* which seeks to achieve its ends by new and sharper teeth in civil rights legislation."

To Wyatt T. Walker in Atlanta, where he served as an aide to Dr. Martin Luther King, the news of the arrests was phoned.

The ranks of the demonstrators had now increased to more than two hundred—mostly high school students.

A hurried call was made to me in Norfolk by Reverend Dunlap. On Thursday, June 6, 1963, I appeared before Judge Calvin Berry in Municipal Court and got the cases continued. For the gathering of evidence and for getting the matter in perspective the then active leadership called a small conference in the office of the Southern Aid Life Insurance Company, where Campbell worked, and included me. (Campbell was later given an unasked-for "Leave Without Pay" by this Negro insurance company.)

Few emotions and attitudes were missing from that conference as sweat poured over bodies harnessed in suits and ties. There was anger because the Reverend Lendell W. Chase had become involved—on the wrong side. Chase, president of the Danville SCLC, had refused to demonstrate and condemned those who had demonstrated. When Dunlap and Campbell had been arrested the day before, leading demonstrations, those they were leading became furious: "Arrest us, too! We are just as guilty as they are!" were the shouts. But there were no arrests. The power structure of Danville was on the "divide them kick" of "just arrest the leaders and all will end."

The viewpoint was practical.

Massive arrests mean massive bonding, massive feeding if bonds are not made, massive trials, and massive attendance of police witnesses during a hot summer when patiences are thin.

Although the "leaders" had been arrested, the demonstration continued on June 5 and grew in intensity, partially because of the lack of direction that leaders could give. *Then* Police Chief Eugene McCain, summoning his experiences of twenty-three years as a cop, decided to send for the Reverend Lendell W. Chase. Chase came. Chase berated those who had demonstrated and ordered them to disperse: "An uncouth gathering doesn't help our cause." A booing was Chase's reward.

There was surprise at this meeting in the insurance office on June 6, 1963, because the arrests had taken place but there was also determination. Two choices were before them, according to the "Wisdom of Dawley": "Demonstrate well, or not at all."

But the positions on either side were not hardened just yet. Hester Womack, a prominent Negro barber and civic leader, indicated that the white Womack on the City Council wanted a further meeting to see if the difficulties could be "worked out."

Within seconds, Arthur Pinchback, the Reverend Lawrence G. Campbell, and the Reverend Alexander Dunlap left the musty oven of an office to be about their personal affairs and also to prepare for the conference with Councilman Womack, Mayor Julian Stinson, and others at City Hall.

Before I left town for Norfolk to pack books, clothing, and office equipment, and to get my affairs in order for a trip by answering mail and returning legal fees collected for cases I no longer had time to handle, I had a brief conference with Harry I. Wood and his wife, Miss Ruth Harvey (who uses her maiden name professionally).

At City Hall, the meeting of June 6, 1963, was doomed before it started.

In attendance for the City was Mayor Stinson, Councilman Charles Womack, City Manager T. E. Temple, Chief Eugene McCain, and Fire Chief Wiseman "Tex" Bray. In attendance for the Movement were Arthur S. Pinchback, Julius Adams, the Reverend L. W. Chase, the Reverend Alexander Dunlap, and Mr. and Mrs. Harry I. Wood.

Getting the meeting off to a bad start, Mayor Stinson questioned the right of people who've been arrested to participate in a committee working on the race problem: "It would not be proper for a person to be arrested one night and placed on a committee the next day."

Certain of those in attendance would leave the conference room for a few minutes and return. And then it was learned.

While the meeting was going on in a conference room on one floor, up on the fourth floor Judge Aiken had issued an injunction naming Pinchback, Adams, Dunlap, and Campbell. Chase was exempted; the hope was that he and Doyle Thomas would oppose the leadership offered by Adams, Dunlap, and Chase.

When the news arrived, the meeting ended abruptly. Adams, Dunlap, and Campbell were uncertain as to which of the white persons in attendance should be designated "Judas."

To King's office in Atlanta the new developments were conveyed.

Among the Movement leaders, hope and desire for

settlement without further demonstrations grew as plans were made for another meeting the next day, "When we've cooled off a little." Friday, June 7, 1963, came.

A special seven-man grand jury was functioning on that Friday.

The newspapers carried two stories of special interest. One was that the United States Court of Appeals of the Fourth Circuit had turned down an appeal to order integration of the Lynchburg Nursing Home for the aged; this appeal was part of the *Lynchburg Omnibus Integration Suit* in which Judge Michie had presided and decided adversely to the interests of the people seeking to make Lynchburg an open city.

A second item—one of rarity—was that Negro citizens in nearby Lexington, N.C., had killed a member of a white mob attacking a Negro housing project.

As the Friday, June 7, meeting progressed during the afternoon with leaders of the Movement and certain of the city officials, again persons kept leaving the room for a few minutes and going upstairs to the meeting of the grand jury.

It happened again. Meetings for negotiation had become too dangerous.

The Reverend Alexander I. Dunlap, the Reverend Lawrence G. Campbell, and Julius Adams had been indicted under a felony charge known as the "John Brown Statute."

"One more meeting with them white folks and we would have been electrocuted," Dunlap shouted in the fullness of his anger over the long distance phone within minutes of learning of the news.

"And that's not poetry," I replied.

At the first meeting the injunction had been handed down which had the effect of almost making it illegal to breathe in Danville. Nothing short of amazement had been the reaction of defense lawyers of the Movement as they saw its language:

The injunction restrains persons from:

Unlawfully assembling in an unauthorized manner on the public streets and in the vicinity of the public buildings of the City of Danville.

Unlawful interference with the lawful operations of private enterprises and businesses in the City of Danville.

Unlawfully obstructing the freedom of movement of the general public of the City of Danville and the general traffic of the City.

Unlawfully obstructing entrances and exits to and from both private business concerns and public facilities in the City of Danville.

Participating in and inciting mob violence, rioting and inciting persons to riot.

Unlawfully carrying deadly weapons, threatening to use such deadly weapons and assaulting diverse citizens of this community.

Unlawfully using loud and boisterous language, interrupting the peace and repose of citizens of this community, business establishments of this community and public works of this community.

Creating and maintaining a public nuisance by reason of unlawful and unauthorized gatherings and loud, boisterous and concerted demonstrations interfering with the peace and quiet and enjoyment of the citizens of the City of Danville.

The second legal stab on the part of Danville, the action of the special grand jury, was more foreboding, the "John Brown Statute":

Section 18. 1-422. *Conspiring to incite the colored population to insurrection against the white population, or the white against the colored.*

If any person conspires with another to incite the colored population of the State to acts of violence and war against the white population or to incite the white population of the State to acts of violence and war against the colored population, he shall, whether such acts of violence and war be made or not, be punished by confinement in the penitentiary not less than five nor more than ten years.

The Sunday, June 9, *Danville Register* concluded that technically this indictment of the three leaders of the Movement "brought to an end a brief but turbulent chapter of racial unrest in the city" but questioned "whether Danville's troubles were just beginning."

Some indication that they were not ending was found in the events of Saturday, June 8.

City Councilman Charles Womack had issued a 3-page statement pleading not to be censured by the City Council on charges alleged to have been made by City Councilman John W. Carter, accusing Womack of undermining the authority of the Corporation Court by discussing racial matters with the Movement leaders while Judge Aiken was issuing an injunction.

Another sign that matters were not ending was found in the nature of the indictments themselves and the black voice of protest the day before from the midst of the members of the special grand jury, the voice of Martin C. Martin, Negro president of Danville's First State Bank.

CHAPTER 6

Whispered Truth

If ye have whispered truth, whisper no longer,
Speak as the tempest does, sterner and stronger.
                                        —Frederick Douglass

"Make it *look* legal" is the rule of thumb employed in the South—and other parts of our nation—when those in control use their control of the police powers to achieve ends once more expeditiously achieved with the flog and the rope.

"L-o-o-k" is the key word.

Sit-in cases involving the leadership of the Danville Movement earlier, in January, 1963, had raised questions about the exclusion of Negroes from Danville juries.

And though Negroes in Danville constitute one-fourth of the population and much less than one-fourth of those on the jury lists, not many eyebrows were lifted in wonderment when a Negro, Martin C. Martin, president of the predominately Negro First State Bank of Danville, was selected for the special grand jury to bring in indictments against the Movement.

Surely Commonwealth Attorney Eugene Link, Police Chief Eugene McCain, Clerk of the Corporation Court T. Tucker, and the others were not disturbed by a Negro's inclusion.

After all, there were six white men on the grand jury,

and unlike petit juries (juries that sit at a trial) no unanimous decision was needed. Any four of the seven could sign a true bill indicting somebody for the alleged commission of a crime.

Furthermore, no one determined to crush racial protest without making one minor concession to the protestors would have considered Martin C. Martin other than a "safe" Negro, i.e., one that could be "trusted."

Martin had lived in Danville practically all of his life, accumulated modest personal security, and made the efficiency of the Negro personnel which ran the bank the pride of Danville and the image it would project of beautiful racial relations.

Not even the fact that Martin was an ardent supporter of the NAACP or the fact that his brother was one of the most aggressive Virginia NAACP lawyers would suggest that he'd do anything to embarrass Danville as it restored "peace" among its Negroes where the City Council patronizingly dealt with "requests" for sidewalks from a colored citizen . . . rather than *demands* that some segregation in public housing be ended now. The Danville City Council, like most communities one can think of, takes literally the phrase "City Fathers."

And who goes to his father and *demands?*

As much as anything else the special grand jury was convened to restore manners to community relations. Since Martin C. Martin was so polite himself, the spokesmen for Dan River Mills, Corning Glass, and the tobacco industry could expect Martin to do the "right" thing.

Martin's physical appearance calmed any lingering fears. His handsome brown features, crowned with a head of gray hair, were of the sort a rich person would like his butler or other trusted servant to have.

But they were wrong.

Martin valued his principles, understood the capacity of the Danville white community to disregard the humanity of the Negro citizen, and wasn't going to agree to things that he considered so basic to his being that no "white friendship" was worth it.

Martin C. Martin, President of the Danville First State Bank, did what is probably unique in the annals of American law, and certainly rare for any Negro living in a place as hellish as Danville. Martin wouldn't sign the indictments filed against Dunlap, Adams, and Campbell, Movement leaders. Instead, he filed a minority report setting forth conduct he observed in the grand jury deliberation and considered to be irregular.

The racist of Danville took a second look at Martin C. Martin as he read his minority report on Saturday, June 8, 1963, in Danville before the other members of the Grand Jury.

Some of the comments made by him about the grand jury proceedings were given in the Danville *Register* of June 9, 1963.

Testimony was permitted to be given to the jury of the alleged hearsay statements from persons or sources which the witness was unwilling and refused to reveal to the jury.

Written memoranda were passed between the foreman and different members at various stages of the hearing, the contents of which were kept secret from the whole jury.

Two members of the jury, Messrs. Nelson Benyunes and John L. Page were permitted to present extensive testimony and personal observations to the other jurors, to influence decisions, without having been previously sworn in as witnesses.

The lone incident on which the indictments were returned which were ruled by the Commonwealth Attorney as being a

violation of the constitutional section under which the indictments were drawn, by undisputed testimony happened in the
absence of one of the defendants, Julius Adams, and I cannot
conscientiously be a part of this indictment under such apparently impossible circumstances.

From undisputed testimony presented also, it seems per-
tinent to me that the attention of the Danville administrative
and executive officers in government should be direct to their
great responsibility to represent fairly, equitably and imparti-
ally all citizens, and give them fair and equal opportunities in
areas under their control.

In this latter point Martin was boring in again on opposition he had met earlier when he suggested that the
grand jury investigate, document and ferret out the racial
segregation prevalent in Danville's government.

Lightning fast, the news spread. Any scorn among
those standing for the practices of segregation was offset
ten-times-ten by the esteem given Martin in the Danville
Negro community. It had been an ugly spot to be in and
Martin had stood tall in a hot sun and cast the sharp
shadow of a man.

"Now I don't want a brother to justify me if I happen
to be wrong, but I do expect him to be with me when I'm
right," was the way that seventy-eight-year-old demonstrator
Daniel McCain put it.

"A man doesn't have to win, just so he fights on the
right side," was James Lee of Detroit's attitude when he
heard of the matter. But there was even more to the minority report.

Mayor Stinson, John W. Carter, Police Chief McCain,
and the representatives of Dan River Mills, through the

public relations officer loaned to the City of Danville—had encouraged the passive white community to remain passive by saying that demonstrators were all crooks, thugs, communists, or idiots. None of these labels would wear well on Martin and no one publicly tried to pin one of them on him. With his minority report Martin C. Martin had in effect sung, "Everybody Wants Freedom."

Following his lead, more of "middle-class" folks let it be known *which side they were on.* On the "D-Day" demonstration which was to occur later, Martin's secretary, the wife of one of his lawyers (who is also a lawyer), Mrs. Maxine Muse, and L. Wilson York, his bank cashier, moved into the line of march and made their witness from behind bars. And there were others.

In between arrests on June 8, 1963, and being bonded out for $5,000 on the insurrection charges, Julius Adams, the Reverend Campbell, and the Reverend Dunlap were burning up the long distance phone lines out of Danville.

The office of Martin Luther King in Atlanta was called and informed of developments and asked for help for its Danville affiliate, the Danville SCLC. Part of the response was to indicate that the newly formed Gandhi Legal Society would take care of all legal matters and expenses of the Danville Movement. The State of Virginia headquarters for the NAACP was contacted. For nitty-gritty field secretaries who could enlist, mobilize, train, and direct the Danville youngsters who would form the backbone of the protest movement, calls were placed to CORE in New York and SNCC in Atlanta. The Danville Movement leaders were informed enough to know that the demonstrations contemplated would involve mostly young people and that

CORE and SNCC were best able to work with the young. Within a few days CORE sent from North Carolina two veterans of nonviolent jungle fighting: Miss Claudia Edwards and Bruce Baines.

On June 8, 1963, the first of the more than eighteen SNCC field secretaries arrived in Danville in time to attend and address the mass meeting being held at the Bibleway Holiness Church. It was Avon Rollins, the most un-SNCC-like person one would ever meet, in the peculiar uniform he wore consisting of a suit, white shirt, four-in-hand tie and white handkerchief neatly folded in the lapel of the suit coat. On the rare occasions when he wore overalls, the SNCC uniform, they were starched and creased and worn with a shirt and tie.

Rollins never looked like anything other than a business executive, which he was. His business was racial protest. Within hours of Avon Rollin's arrival, plans were made for Monday's demonstrations and the additional SNCC personnel was on the way.

Much of Sunday, June 9, was spent contacting wire services and news media about the Danville protest. Their response was less than enthusiastic.

There are some days unlike all other days, days which achieve a special significance because of some good event or because of a heinous incident which sears the date into minds and evokes emotions that are not easily dissipated by the most profound logic. It's not sufficient to say: "Don't think about it. Forget it. Let the past be the past."

For Americans such a date is December 7, 1941, when Pearl Harbor was attacked, precipitating millions of deaths.

For Danville such a date is June 10, 1963 . . . the day which lawyer Sam W. Tucker referred to in his eloquent plea for justice from a Danville Federal Court as "A day of infamy."

It began like a lot of other hot days in June, with the sun rising early and standing in the doorway of the horizon. Early risers who picked their copies of the Danville *Register* from their porches or apartment hallways probably didn't pay much attention to the front-page story announcing that Governor Wallace had sworn to stand in the doorway of the University of Alabama to block admission of two Negroes. If the Negro boycott of Danville newspapers had not been in operation and the SNCC field secretaries in town, or enroute to Danville, had read the Danville *Bee* they wouldn't have paid special attention to the little box in the paper which stated:

STAY AWAY. Mayor Julian R. Stinson issued a statement this afternoon urging all citizens of Danville to stay away from any area where a demonstration threatens.

No one in CORE or the local Movement leadership would have paid special attention or noted that this was the first time such a statement had been made by the city administration since the beginning of the protest. As a matter of fact, such an announcement might have found welcome because it would in effect cause white citizens to join the Negro community's boycott of downtown merchants since this is where all of the demonstrations had been held—in the heart of the business district.

Shortly after 4:00 A.M. that morning Daniel Foss, Brandeis University student of sociology and SNCC field secretary, arrived, and joined Avon Rollins at the home of Mrs. Beatrice Hairston.

At 10:00 A.M. Rollins and Foss left the Hairston home

and went downtown to the Spring Street Municipal Parking lot to meet the demonstrators. There were about sixty of them gathered there; most were teen-agers.

Minutes before 11:00 A.M. the demonstrators began the march, chanting and singing through the downtown streets for the better part of an hour. They were in perfect—almost military—order. Their leaders appeared to be Ernest Howard Smith, a Negro taxi cab driver in his forties, Ezell Barksdale, seventeen, a short, dark brownskin fellow who was the same size as Smith . . . and Thurmond Echols, sixteen.

Echols is a high school honor student who had provided excellent leadership on practically every demonstration held. Much of the recruiting of the high school students to join the demonstrations was provided by this apt young man. And this leadership carried over into other than demonstrations. At the rallies held nightly Thurmond Echols would lead cheers and freedom songs with appropriate waves of a white cotton cap.

The demonstrators massed near the top of the steps of the City Hall and began to sing. A few made cracks about the statue of George Wooding, the Confederate hero: "Say, we got one white man up here with us, but he doesn't look too happy. Guess we won't ask him to speak." White clerical workers in the office windows of the Municipal Building were horrified at the "disrespectful comment" made about Danville's saint.

The police, who had surrounded and followed the demonstrators since the beginning of the march, then seized Echols, Barksdale, and Smith and pulled them into the building to be booked. The remainder of the demonstrators surged into the alley, that convenient and awful alley, between the City Hall, where the three arrested persons were, and the jail.

Captain Boswell proclaimed the gathering to be a riot.

"Persons who don't clear this area at once will be arrested," barked Boswell, and gestured to his fellow Danville policemen to move away from the demonstrators in the alley.

Moments later the demonstrators were washed out of the convenient and awful alley between the jail and City Hall with jets of water from fire hoses.

Enraged and terrified, the demonstrators fled toward Spring Street, which houses the six or seven stores that constitute Danville's Negro business district.

The police swooped down and began indiscriminately arresting Negroes on the street, including spectators who emerged from the small stores to observe the chaotic situation. Paeans of praise for the "efficient" Danville police blurted forth at frequent intervals over the local radio stations within moments, fortifying the passiveness of the white community. But the word in the Negro community was different. Negro shopkeepers spread their eyewitness accounts to customers and others.

Some forty-eight were arrested immediately and a new phase of Danville "justice" began. Thurmond Echols, sixteen, was within the purview of juvenile laws. He was encouraged to call his mother and tell her he was in jail. The police asked her to come down and get him. Upon arrival at the jail she was arrested. The charge was contributing to the delinquency of a minor by failing to supervise properly and prevent him from violating Danville's laws. Echol's mother was allowed to make a call. She called her husband and asked that he get money and come bail her out. Mr.

Echols, the husband, came to jail to get his wife. He was jailed on the same charge of "contributing to the delinquency of a juvenile charge." Mother, father, and son were in jail—"togetherness."

For the other demonstrators seventeen or younger the same procedure was followed.

Avon Rollins and Foss were arrested while trying to take pictures of the arrests.

Around 4:00 P.M. June 10, 1963, the male prisoners were moved to the Danville City Farm where they were to remain for three days. On orders of the white powers-that-be, no one was permitted to make bonds or post bail—a matter of concern to few except the Negro community and the cook at the City Farm, who had to prepare additional meals consisting of a bowl of grits for breakfast, two bologna sandwiches for lunch, and supper per man.

It is difficult to explain the menu—or lack of it—at the City Farm other than the profit. Vegetable gardens, a dairy, and a meat processing plant for the beef cattle raised are maintained with the prison labor. Meat is seen in the prison food only on the rare occasions when there is a stew. Milk becomes available when an inspection is imminent by an "outsider."

Like most of the other facilities operated by Danville, the City Farm is racially segregated. Two-thirds of the capacity for the Farm is allocated for Negro prisoners in an area where Negroes constitute but one-fourth of the population.

For the Negro prisoners at the farm the atmosphere is less than congenial. This spills over to Negro lawyers and others who come to the institution in non-prisoner roles. I saw a Negro lawyer viciously jabbed with a broad key to get his attention and to show him where seats were that could be utilized while his client was "brought up front."

The farm also holds a terror for whites. A white prisoner given a choice of pleading guilty to a misdemeanor and serving twelve months on the Farm or pleading guilty to a felony and pulling eighteen months in the State Penitentiary quickly chooses the penitentiary.

At 5:10 P.M. June 10, 1963, two SNCC field secretaries, Bob Zellner and his beautiful wife-to-be, Dorothy Miller, arrived in Danville.

At 7:03 P.M. Ivanhoe Donaldson, another SNCC field secretary, arrived and was arrested after asking a cop for directions to the High Street Baptist Church. The charge: operating a car with faulty hand brakes.

Later the same evening Bruce Baine, CORE field secretary, arrived from North Carolina. Cordell Reagon and his wife Bernice, SNCC Freedom Singers, arrived to take part in the Movement—this is part of a plan to allow the singers to intersperse concert tours with field work.

A mass meeting was begun about 8:30 P.M. at the Bibleway Holiness Church where some of those beaten and roughly handled during the afternoon demonstration, but not arrested, "told the story."

Headed by the Reverend Hildreth McGhee, fifty volunteers—mostly ladies—left the mass meeting to conduct a prayer vigil for the demonstrators inside jail. After a 2-mile walk from the church solemnly singing "Jesus Keep Me Near the Cross," the group arrived in front of the jail.

In that awful and convenient alley between the City Hall and the jail the Reverend McGhee knelt in prayer.

Bob Zellner was arrested for snapping the picture of Chief McCain as he approached. Policemen and deputized white males adorned with new truncheons sealed off one end of the alley. The other end was blocked by Danville firemen with hoses and pressure on. Six firemen held the front of each of the hoses.

On one side of the demonstrators was the back wall of the City Hall. On the other side was the front wall of the jail.

First the high-pressured nozzles spewed water with explosive force into the alley. And then came the clubs. Beatings followed. The convenience of the alley was fully used—by the hands bearing the clubs.

One of the ladies beaten that night, who bears a permanent scar where her face was crushed, Mrs. Mary Thomas, filed suit against some of the Danville officials. In a section of the suit called a "Summation of the Pleadings" the events of that night in the alley were related somewhat poetically:

Conceive of a nightmare.

Hear the discordant screams of fear borne of a belief that death will come on the next blow slammed into a body so inflamed with swelling and pain that the finality of death would be a relief.

Let that discordant sound be punctuated by a thousand thuddings caused by hard clubs sinking into soft skulls and flesh . . . as the muscular arms of police and deputized-garbage-truck-drivers flail. Wonder why such unprovoked heinousness occurred as you smell the blood of the overcrowded emergency room of Danville's segregated Winslow Hospital.

See the slaughter-pen effect created by a sticky human blood from gashed heads and bodies which is smeared everywhere: clothing, floors, doors, tables, seats . . .

This did happen in Danville in the State of Virginia on the night of June 10th, 1963. Subsequent events have shown that those City officials responsible for this living-nightmare-come-true are ashamed. Subsequent events have also indicated that they were amazed at their own capacity in demonstrating how inhuman man can be to his fellowman.

But the body, mind and soul of this plaintiff—and others who suffered similarly—are scarred forever . . . and so is the soul of Danville.

Money cannot repair this damage. It can only pay the medical bills, and partially compensate for the loss of income and inconvenience resulting from Danville's night of infamy. This is a night that Danville will never try to remember, but can never forget. For this wrongful conduct the defendants are being asked by this suit to render some justice to those whom they have wronged in a way that no one should ever be wronged.

There were 50 who marched that night; 47 required medical treatment. Back injuries, lacerated scalps, bruised shoulders, broken wrists and feet, were all part of the list of injuries plus concussions.

Having heard of the reported beating, a fellow with a rich Mississippi drawl, Newton Hustead, called the office of the Danville City Manager asking an explanation. A lady working in the office gave him an explanation, "It was horrible but justified." She then highlighted the southern hospitality that is so important: "But we never sent a bill for medical expenses to any of them."

The 35-bed Winslow Hospital is both segregated and publicly owned. It is hardly larger than an ordinary clinic— and for colored only.

Three doctors had worked until daybreak treating the onslaught of injuries. The treatment was at the expense of the city; no one was billed. Generosity?

CHAPTER 7

Inconvenience and Concern

Rock-a-bye baby, high on the tree
Nobody knows the hell I see.

Though you ba-a-ah like a goat
Supper times come they'll cut a throat.

Rock Baby!
. . . High on that damned tree
Nobody—but nobody!
Knows the hell I see.
                    —A "Holler" by Dawley

Different people had different responses to the Night
of Infamy, June 10, 1963.

The regular meeting of the City Council was held the
following day, June 11, 1963, and Councilman Womack
successfully defended himself from censure with an emotional plea for understanding because his efforts at working
on token concessions were not intended to reflect upon anybody, especially the court and Judge Aiken. The newspaper
said that Councilman John Carter distinguished himself at
the meeting by justifying the beatings of the Negro demonstrators and coining a new phrase for Danville: "Raging
Mau Mau riots."

But there were variations in the white power complex. Apparently Mayor Stinson and Police Chief McCain

sensed how much of a miracle had happened because there were no deaths.

Mayor Stinson was quoted as saying: "I'm not happy the incident occurred. It would have been a horrible thing had it been separated from all the rest that has occurred." To the same effect were the remarks of Chief McCain: "Speaking of last night's violence, my men were tired and their nerves were on edge. They were not acting in their best capacity."

In the Danville Negro community there was a single reaction of smoldering hate that hung like funk—and the *City Hall* knew it. Thirty state troopers were moved into the City under the command of Capt. J. W. Burrows on June 11, 1963, and armed with repeater shotguns, tear-gas guns, and an armored tank. Vice-Mayor George B. Anderson called for a voluntary curfew and the white community wondered: Would the heinousness of the police the night before cause the hatred of the Danville Negroes to erupt and spew forth? Would the Danville Negroes seek revenge because they had been reminded by the beatings that America had by some logic made it a capital offense to be born black?

A demonstration began in the early part of the afternoon of June 11. In two ways it was different from previous demonstrations: there were bandaged and crippled Negroes, beaten the night before, hobbling in the line of marching demonstrators—blood oozed through the gauze compresses; inhumanity expressed under cover of darkness was being shown in the sunlight. Moreover, the Reverend Lendell W. Chase was leading the demonstration, his first such effort.

Chase is the pastor of the High Street Baptist Church of Danville, the Baptist church you would join if you wanted your church membership to give you "status." Even though operative, this myth was still just that— a myth. The preacher's pay was so inadequate that Chase spent considerable time searching for substitute teaching work in nearby counties and towns (his role in the Danville *Omnibus Integration Suit* as a plaintiff disqualified him from such income from the Danville schools).*

In physical appearance Chase, a short and rotund man, is not too impressive—until you hear the near perfect diction and rolling baritone of his voice, which would be an asset to an actor. He is the president of the Danville SCLC. In and out of that capacity, he had been critical of the demonstrations led against his wishes by others in the affiliate: Dunlap, Campbell, and Adams. The evidence was conflicting as to whether Chase's position was correct. But Chase was astute.

He knew that his position in the Negro community had been compromised.

He realized on June 11, that it was a mistake to have gone a few days earlier, June 5, to the steps of City Hall at the bidding of Chief McCain and to have asked the demonstrators to leave. The demonstrators knew what had been done prior to Chase's being called by the police—they had seen the force used . . . the twisting of arms and the grabbing of Dunlap and Campbell by the belt and pulling so that their pants cut into their crotches.

And then the beatings had been inflicted. Both emotions and intellect told Chase that prior reservations and judgments about demonstrations were no longer valid.

So on June 11, 1963, Chase led demonstrators back to the steps of the City Hall after the Night of Infamy, and the bronze image of Danville's hero, George Wooding, was once again honored by the presence of defiant Danville Negroes singing—though softer than before—"Everybody Wants Freedom."

* On January 3, 1965, he announced his resignation to accept a better-paying church job in Virginia Beach, Virginia.

Still there was something about Chase on the demonstration he led after the beatings that clung to the "old order." Chase had believed City Hall when their spokesmen (the two Danville daily papers) had encouraged the passive white population to believe that the arrests occurred only because "the singing was loud and disturbed the businessmen and people had been pushed off the sidewalk and streets blocked by demonstrators."

Obsession-like, Chase made sure that the sixty persons in his demonstration crossed only when the lights favored them, and walked in twos on the sidewalk and to one side.

After two silent marches around the jail and City Hall, Chase led the demonstrators on a march from the jail to the Bibleway Church, a distance of more than two miles. The injured rode in cars.

Chase further showed his naiveté when interviewed by reporters: "This demonstration led by me is not to condone anything that happened earlier. In part, it was to prove that we can conduct a peaceful demonstration."

Chase was praised.

Both newspapers found an opportunity in the subsequent stories on June 11, which condemned earlier demonstrations, to applaud his leadership. The power structure wanted a certain effect to flow from the praise of Chase and the failure of the police to arrest him.

They got what they wanted.

The division that remained between the leadership of the Reverend Chase and the Reverend Doyle Thomas on one hand, and that of Julius Adams, the Reverend Lawrence Campbell, and the Reverend Alexander Dunlap on the other hand, was the effect wanted. The hand of Chase had been strengthened. The result of his one experience had put him in the position to think that, "The arrests of the persons prior to this date were their own fault."

Doubts about the matter were cleared up when Chief McCain had explained why there had been no arrest on June 11 of the demonstrators led by Chase: "I feel that so long as the Reverend Mr. Chase leads them, the demonstrations will continue peaceful. I have known Chase to be a responsible spokesman for Negroes whose word can be relied upon."

But there was one thing that had gone unnoticed.

With motion picture and still cameras, at the behest of the *City Hall*, policemen had preserved a record of every demonstrator . . . for a rendezvous with destiny and the City Farm, on a date of *City Hall*'s choosing.

Flowing into the City at this time were the eyes and ears of the nation: NBC, CBS, and ABC television; UPI, AP, and INS news services; prominent papers such as the Washington *Post*, the Washington *Evening Star* and the *Christian Science Monitor*.

Meanwhile, Councilman Womack cancelled plans for future biracial talks and took off for the West Coast on vacation.

In recognition of the presence of the national news media, Danville began a campaign of vilification of the demonstrators. Reports were prepared to show the arrest records of the local people arrested for demonstrating while simultaneously local newspapers characterized the national civil rights organizations involved as "communist-inspired."

Events developed rapidly elsewhere in Danville on June 11, while the Reverend Lendell Chase was leading the demonstrators. In the company of James Forman, the executie director of SNCC, Leo Branton had arrived in Danville from Jackson, Miss. Hours later Danny Lyons, SNCC photographer, ambled into town with a small black suitcase and a small black camera bag.

Branton is a prosperous trial lawyer from Los Angeles

noted for his handling of personal injury cases and libel suits involving movie stars and entertainers. After a brief conversation with James Forman, Branton joined two of the local Negro attorneys in an effort to get bail set for the seventy-six persons being held without bail and, failing that, to get medical attention for Charles Echols, who was in danger of losing the sight of one eye. Echols had been one of the fifty persons marching in the nighttime demonstration. On both counts they failed.

It was hard to tell which of the three lawyers looked saddest after being told there would be no bail: Andrew C. Muse, Jerry Williams, or Leo Branton. As for the request to be able to provide medical attention for the grotesquely swollen eye of Echols, they were informed: "He's all right. The city doc will look at him when he gets a chance."

It was hard, hard to remain cool, hard to remain functional. But Muse, Williams, and Branton did remain functional—though not cool. Up they went to Muse's office above the First State Bank and there, along with Sam W. Tucker, roughed-out a *habeas corpus* petition for filing the next day.

Danny Lyons went about his business, recording reality with a battered 35 mm camera that produced prints so vivid that one can't help being engulfed in the emotion portrayed. Everywhere I went that day I heard the incessant snap of the camera's film-advancing lever flinging itself out of Danny's way.

There was no need to guess at what James Forman would do in Danville. A month before, in May, I had seen him do it in Birmingham: utilize his ability to command the respect of his fellow SNCC workers and other young people to change a situation of bedlam into something no worse than chaos. In Birmingham, every day shortly after 1:00 P.M. the demonstrators would march out of the church and proceed fifty yards, get arrested, and be carried away in a yellow Jefferson County school bus.

Forman had changed this. Late the night of his first day in Birmingham he had argued the viewpoint: "We want results. To get results the white citizens of Birmingham must become concerned about our problem and, perhaps, even be inconvenienced by that problem. Marching a few yards, being arrested, all within the confines of the ghetto, isn't conducive to developing the concern of white people who'll know nothing about our plight except what they see on television."

James Lee, of Detroit, and I, who had been permitted in the Birmingham conference, looked at each other in amazement. We were both hoping that nothing about the legal status of the Gadsden, Alabama, *Omnibus Integration Suit* would develop the following morning to prevent us from being in Birmingham to "see the happenings."

The pattern of the Birmingham demonstrations had become regular. The pattern of the police action had become regular. The demonstrators didn't leave the church until after 1:00 P.M. to march a few yards. The cops didn't come on duty until noon, and made the arrests as swiftly as possible ("save the rough stuff for jail where there are no cameramen around"). The demonstrations had become a game with fixed rules. Forman changed the rules.

Word went out that as many people as possible were to be at the church as close to 8:00 A.M. as they could arrange. As groups came that next morning into Birmingham's Sixteenth Street Baptist Church, they were quickly searched, given forms to fill out, orientated and told to leave the church at once in small groups of twos or threes, go to designated parking lots downtown, look in parked cars and get signs, conceal the signs, go to Pizits, Loveman's or one

of the other stores, and at the blowing of the noon whistle
—sit down in an aisle!

Before noon 500 young people had infiltrated downtown Birmingham. At noon 500 people sat in aisles, door-
ways, and other places.

Birmingham panicked.

The cops gathering lackadaisically in front of the church
at noon panicked and hurtled themselves toward downtown
Birmingham on motorcycles and in cars.

When the police in front of the church left for downtown, 2,000 persons gathered in the church followed the
police—downtown. Along the way they were joined by
others.

An hour or so later a mighty chorus of singing and
chanting Negroes triumphantly marched back from downtown singing "Glory, Glory Hallelujah" and other Freedom
songs. In between, every major business in downtown Birmingham had been inoperative at what ordinarily would
have been their busiest hour.

Birmingham's white population became concerned
about the Birmingham Negroes' problem—because they had
been inconvenienced by it.

And that had been the last demonstration in Birmingham. Within hours Dr. Martin Luther King and Fred Shuttlesworth reached their famous agreement with the merchants.

So I had some idea of what James Forman would do in
Danville on Tuesday, June 11, 1963.

After brief exchanges of greetings with me, Forman,
Cordell Reagon, and Ivanhoe Donaldson—all of SNCC—
headed for the hill where the High Street Baptist Church sat.
They were about to begin.

It was now time for me to begin.

CHAPTER 8

Day After Infamy

An old white woman recalled exactly
How Nat crept down the steps, axe in hand,
After murdering a woman and child in bed,
"Right in this house at the head of these stairs."
(In a house built long after Nat was dead.)

She pointed to a brick store where Nat was captured,
(Nat was taken in a swamp, three miles away)
With his men around him, shooting from the windows
(She was thinking of Harper's Ferry and old John Brown.)

She cackled as she told how they riddled Nat with bullets
(Nat was tried and hanged at Courtland, ten miles away)
She wanted to know why folks would come miles
Just to ask about an old nigger fool.
                    —Sterling Brown, "Remembering Nat Turner"

"Goodbye, Snake," Cordell Reagon said as he and the others went on their way in front of Oliver's Cafe on Spring Street. Pensively, I sauntered toward the offices above the First State Bank where a critical meeting was to be held on the matter of legal representation. It was set for 5:00 P.M. in the office of Lawyer Muse. (In the south the custom among Negroes is to make a title out of the word "Lawyer" as most people use the word "Doctor.")

Muse's office was air-conditioned, and because I was

sweating from the immobilizing dry heat of temperatures in the 90's I found myself chilled—pleasantly so. It was then that I became most aware of the climatic conditions that anger, fear, and worry had caused me to forget prior to arrival in Muse's office.

Reflecting both good taste and good income—from a law practice and wise investments—the law office was well appointed, the papers on the desks were in orderly piles, the hardwood tops on the desks had been polished to a sheen that made the wood feel soft and spongy to the touch of my hand.

The air was fresh and clean feeling to my nostrils with a slight fragrance in it that was delicate yet masculine. (An innovation of his efficient secretary, Miss Delores Page.)

That office on that day will always be fresh in my mind; that meeting in that office seems to have changed the course of my life and the course of the lives of hundreds of others in Danville. And by this I have reference to more than projection created by the protest which caused the inclusion of the *Kunstler Statute* in the Civil Rights Bill of 1964.* I mean more than that, even though that provision may have been enough to justify decisions to forego the vacations and to go into the vineyard and labor in Danville for a harvest promised for those who nourish the tree of Liberty. I refer to the personal tragedies and triumphs in the lines of a thousand Danville citizens who labored in the belief that if we labored long enough, and well enough, we could not fail.

We were the *true believers.*

For some, for far too many, the belief was that the harvest would come when the promises made by Dr. Martin Luther King to come into Danville with his "task force" would be carried out—as everyone knew he would—and

---

* For text, see p. 232.

then Danville would become the Birmingham of the upper South.

For many more the sweet taste of victory would come whenever there could be that confrontation between the United States and the City of Danville. For surely if we just told our story we would get help: "Aren't the Constitution and God on our side?"

For a small few there were no dreams either of King or the federal government: "Dan River Mills runs this town. Segregation will end here when Dan River Mills says so—no sooner, no later. Ways must be found to make the concern of Danville Negroes the concern of Dan River Mills. To inconvenience Dan River Mills is to make it concerned. A way must be found to boycott."

As I waited in that office on that day, June 11, 1963, these beliefs weighed heavily upon me. I know now that I made the right decision—even though I and thirteen others may ultimately spend years in the penitentiary convicted under the "John Brown" law. If, as the white power structure of Danville suggests, contributing to the Danville protest against racial segregation as an overworked and unpaid lawyer constitutes such a crime, I must plead before their altars: Guilty!

And may their gods have mercy on their souls.

The people gathered in that office, at that time, were an impressive collection of part of the black power in Virginia. Chitchatting and acting and speaking in a forced casualness was W. Lester Banks, Executive Secretary of the Virginia association of NAACP chapters—the best organized collection of chapters of the NAACP in America.

Sitting in Muse's chair behind Muse's desk was Sam W. Tucker, attorney. Tucker wore two "hats," both of which represented power and therefore money. He was acting chairman of the Legal Redress Committee of the Virginia State NAACP, a collection of fifteen lawyers throughout the State who handled cases for the NAACP. His other "hat" was that of representative of the NAACP Legal Defense Educational Fund, Inc., a tax-exempt corporation with an annual budget in excess of a million dollars.

Present were four of the five local Negro attorneys of Danville (all of whom were part of the Virginia NAACP team of lawyers), Miss Ruth Harvey, head of the Danville NAACP team, Harry I. Wood, Jerry Williams, and Andrew C. Muse.

Representing the Danville Movement were the Reverend Lawrence G. Campbell and the Reverend Alexander I. Dunlap. And then there were Leo Branton of Los Angeles and myself.

After some small talk and polite greetings, Leo Branton pushed to the heart of the legal needs as he saw them:

"I hope you won't think me too presumptuous for beginning the discussion, but it may be best that I do so, simply because I'm not local and have no axe to sharpen." Everyone's attention fixed on Branton.

"I've never seen any of you before—except Len who travels over the country making speeches and singing about Southern struggles. My only ties with the South are my birth in Arkansas and that my brother, Wiley, is an active NAACP lawyer in that state." Banks and Muse looked surprised.

Branton continued. "I just happen to be in Danville because I was in Jackson with Jim Forman and he asked me to make the trip to Danville with him that I might be of some service. In all my years as a lawyer I've never seen matters so desperate as in Danville. I don't need to tell you. You've seen everything I've seen. My stomach is still sick

from the sight of those women and girls whose heads were
gashed and bloody. That hospital was a sight that every
American should see." Aside from an occasional clearing of
the throat, no one said a word except Branton.

"These people need help; they need help at once and
plenty of it, and I just don't know of anyone or any organization with the ability to respond to that need except the
NAACP."

Branton ended. Sam Tucker and Lester Banks seemed
more relaxed than when the discussion started.

"What help will you give to the people here in Danville?" Reverend Campbell quickly asked. Tucker responded.

"I haven't fully discussed this matter with Jack, Jack
Greenberg of the NAACP Legal Defense Fund, but I believe
that he would be willing to underwrite all of the legal expenses of the Danville protest. Lawyers, court reporters,
transcripts, filing fees, briefs, everything. And what he won't
handle I have the distinct feeling that the Virginia State
NAACP would take."

The offer was impressive, seemed generous and was re-
lieving because it meant that I wouldn't be needed and all
my cancelled plans could be reinstated. It would never
have occurred to me at that time to question anything about
the offer or to question why the Virginia State officials had
massed themselves so quickly: the Presidents of the Virginia
State Branches, the Reverend Francis Griffin of Prince
Edward County fame, Sam Tucker, who was the top NAACP
legal man in the State, and W. Lester Banks, who was the
Executive Secretary of the state organization.

But questions did occur to Campbell.

"Suppose we, the Movement, decide to demonstrate.
Would we be bound to confer with the NAACP lawyers
first?" Campbell asked.

Tucker answered. "It would be expected that some conferring would take place. Since the NAACP will be footing the bills, we would want to be able to caution against anything unwise. But you got to remember, I want Freedom, too. And years ago, before it was as popular as it is now, my brother and I were involved in what may have been Virginia's first library sit-in."

"What about Len, the Snake Doctor? Will he be one of the lawyers? Will this team of NAACP lawyers work with him?" Campbell probingly asked.

The questions shocked me into a tense state. For years my partners, Joe Jordan and Ed Dawley, and I had been fighting the things we considered to be wrong about the NAACP: its conservativeness, saying "No" to all cases except school integration cases, for the most part, and refusing to raise the question of courtroom segregation at *every* criminal trial were but two examples. Furthermore I didn't consider myself indispensable to Danville. Tucker answered, apologetically—in the way that I knew he would answer.

"NAACP money can only go to NAACP lawyers and Holt isn't in that category."

The room became silent.

Breathing could be heard mixed in with the hum of the air conditioner.

In my mind a thousand million thoughts raced; all of them dwelled around announcing, then and there, that the Danville Movement didn't need me. There had been a lot of communities where protest had been made throughout the south where my only connection was to read about it in the *Afro-American* or *Jet*.

And then it happened.

Just when I would have spoken those words of withdrawal, refused to participate in Danville, and left the Dan-

ville Movement with no choice other than to go with the
NAACP offer of complete legal aid—and control, it hap-
pened. W. Lester Banks, Executive Secretary of the Virginia
State Association of NAACP Branches, spoke.

"As I see it, Danville is just like the people were in
Prince Edward County when we came in and helped them
in 1951."

That did it.

That remark made me know that all the plans I had for
that summer had to be damned and discarded.

My thoughts flowed back over the past deeds of the
NAACP and its representatives gathered near me. I discarded the cloak of broadmindedness and charity I had worn
into that room. Danville could not be left to the NAACP.

I remembered Prince Edward County, Va., the only
place in the English-speaking world where the public schools
had been closed for four years. I remembered that for a
whole year the fine and rich NAACP did nothing, absolutely
nothing, to justify the faith of the thousands of black boys
and girls who were denied all schooling and who had, at the
insistence of the NAACP, declined offers for private segregated education. I remembered that the schools were closed
in September of 1959 and that it was not until a year later,
in 1960, that any action was taken to force the reopening
of the schools. I remembered that this action in 1960 was
precipitated when it was thought that the firm of Jordan,
Dawley, and Holt was going to file actions in federal court
that the NAACP should have filed a year before.

Then my thoughts went to the Reverend Francis
Griffin, now Virginia State NAACP President, who as leader
of Prince Edward County had stymied a nearly executed
1962 sit-in of Prince Edward County students in Congress.
I remembered that while Griffin was leading Prince

Edward County and thousands of the children of laborers, poor farmers and other poor persons who had no schools, he informed me in Lynchburg in the spring of 1962 that his children were attending school in New Jersey.

I also remembered the attempts by the Virginia NAACP to discourage the New Year's Day Pilgrimage to Richmond for Civil Rights on at least two occasions.

And I remembered the case of *Sam W. Tucker* vs. *Commonwealth*, the same Tucker sitting before me. I remembered how he had been brought before a racially inspired committee and accused of improper conduct as a lawyer—and censured. I remembered how that same NAACP, which was then offering to defend hundreds in Danville, whom it knew not, had failed to take the case of Sam W. Tucker, whom it knew well, before the United States Supreme Court. I considered this unconscionable. I felt that the Supreme Court, without taking a second whiff, would smell the stench of racial segregation in the disciplinary action taken against Tucker, and with one swish cleanse his record of the onus of having been disciplined.

Before I could speak, and before anyone else could speak, Dunlap and Campbell spoke. Their message was clear: "Len Holt, Ol' Snaky, is the Movement lawyer. If you want to put some people here to work with him, good. Otherwise, we're sorry."

In a most pleasant way, I was stunned; I was overwhelmed . . . silently, in an act of conscience, I accepted a role that had to be fulfilled.

Afterwards Tucker explained to the local Danville lawyers that even though the Movement didn't accept the offer, the NAACP would defend an individual person who came to it and asked for help. There were worried looks on every face.

Mine too had a worried look.

To understand the source of my worry, one must understand the time and costs of justice in America and Virginia.

Some of the time and costs factors of defending Movement cases are the following:

Individual trials. Even though one is the "Movement lawyer," the relationship that exists in the courtroom is between the individual charged with a crime and his lawyer. As a lawyer one is obligated to do what is best for the individual, not necessarily what may be best for the Movement. Happily, in most instances the Movement interest and the interest of the individual are the same. Generally, individual trials serve best the individual.

On a protest march down the main streets of Danville there may have been two hundred people marching. All two hundred would have been arrested and charged with such things as disorderly conduct, parading without a permit, violation of some court injunction, obstructing traffic, resisting arrest, and contributing to the delinquency of a minor.

In spite of the desire for military precision and discipline, seldom does a protest movement get it—at least not in every demonstration. The factual situation, what each person is doing or is seen doing by a policeman, will vary immensely. For example, take the charge of resisting arrest. The command of a particular policeman to the group may not have been said with such volume so as to have been heard in the rear of the ranks. Hence, if it can be proven that they didn't hear, they should not be fined or imprisoned because they went in a direction other than the one designated by the police officer.

Each charge dropped means less time that the individual may have to serve, less fine that he or his family may have to pay, and less bond money tied up. In addition the time of the lawyer is freed for other cases.

The mere fact that individual trials may clog up the criminal courts, postpone the dates of conviction and appeals for others in the Movement, or that the police may be inconvenienced is not a matter that ever guides the consideration of a defense attorney.

Court reporters. When a person of means is arrested his lawyer immediately gets the services of a court reporter who will appear at the court and record the testimony.

Almost no police court, municipal court, justice of the peace court, magistrate's court or court where preliminary hearings of felony charges and minor criminal offenses are tried, has its own court reporter. The accused person must furnish his own court reporter and pay him.

In Virginia there are usually two trials for an offense. The first one is in the police court or before a justice of the peace. If the accused is found guilty and appeals he will have another trial before a *court of record.* In Virginia these courts are usually Circuit Courts or Corporation Courts. (In the federal judicial system they are called District Courts.)

At both trials there should be a court reporter. The average cost of the court reporter and a copy of the testimony he takes will run roughly more than $200 for both trials.

This is one money factor. Multiply it by the number of persons arrested or the number of charges arising out of a Movement. In Danville for instance there were more than 700 persons arrested and the number of charges pressed against them exceeded 1300.

Appeal costs. Appealing a conviction from a *court of record* to the highest court of the state—usually called the State

Supreme Court or the Court of Appeals—involves more money.

The clerk of the *court of record* gets a fee for preparing a record and sending it to the Supreme Court of the state. That record consists of the original or copies of the motions filed by both sides, the warrant of arrest, and exhibits such as pictures, picket signs, and the transcript of testimony.

The clerk of the Court of Appeals or State Supreme Court requires a fee for filing the case. He requires another fee for printing in booklet form the record from the court below. In many states one has to post an appeal bond from which costs incurred are subtracted. Finally, there is the cost of printing the briefs. A brief is a printed pamphlet giving the reasons of the appealing party why the State Supreme Court should endorse or change results reached by the court below.

Miscellaneous expenditures. Depending on the case and the facts these costs may mount. Sometimes pictures have to be bought, exhibits made, travel costs for witnesses paid, or certified statements of populations or other official information must be purchased. For example, defense of the people involved in the Movement in Danville, at one point, required the purchase of back copies of the two daily papers for a period of two months.

Feeding the lawyers. Though cases may seem to be simple questions of "either I did it or I didn't," I've never yet seen a good lawyer who rested his case with proof of that simple fact.

When the number of charges are in excess of a thousand or two thousand spread over a period of months or the number of persons arrested are in the hundreds, what money, if any, should be paid to the lawyers involved for their services?

Should their labor be donated?

Or if they are paid, what should be the rate of payment for the time rendered?

Unless and until the position is successfully taken that those who engage in protest against racial segregation will not defend themselves in court when arrested and accept whatever fines and sentences are given, lawyers will be needed. On the few occasions that the total jail and no bail practice has been tried the judges have increased the size of the sentences and fines.

Campbell, Dunlap, and I left Muse's office together on June 11, 1964, and we talked. Our talk had that strange mixture of wonderment, bravado, and fear common when one has made a strong and principled decision that may have permanently severed a bridge that one isn't sure he won't want to cross back over when the results of the strong and principled decision are measured by an unforeseen crisis, or from an historical perspective.

Good, bad, or indifferent—for better or worse, the NAACP and its money offer had been rejected.

That decision had been made by Dunlap and Campbell partially because they had confidence in me; I had already served them a year. It had also been made partially because of their own suspicions of and experiences with the NAACP.

With good reason they knew that accepting the offer of June 11, 1963, would have meant accepting the control and influence of Jack Greenberg, who, in his office at 10 Columbus Circle, maintains very tight strings over those using the funds of his NAACP Legal Defense Fund. They knew that at every planning conference on strategy or demonstrations the guidance of W. Lester Bank of the State NAACP office and Roy Wilkins would restrain. Dunlap and Campbell had not forgotten that these same people had fought them before within the NAACP and that because of these fights they, Dunlap and Campbell, had withdrawn from the NAACP and formed a local chapter in Danville of SCLC. Nothing had happened, so far, to persuade them that forsaking the NAACP had been a mistake.

These Movement leaders had suspicions and fears that they—Dunlap, Campbell, and Adams—might become as expendable to the NAACP as the schoolless children in Prince Edward County, Va. At that point, June 11, 1963, they were the only three persons facing ten years of confinement under the "John Brown" law. There was justifiable concern that the protesting, the protesting organization, and its leadership continue—until exoneration.

But there was more than misgivings about the NAACP.

There was a strong and abiding faith in Wyatt T. Walker, administrative aid to Martin Luther King; there was unlimited confidence in King himself, and there was respect for the image and power of the Southern Christian Leadership Conference headed by King. After all, hadn't they borne the burden in the heat of day in Birmingham and delivered a symbol unto America that was energizing liberal whites and Negroes everywhere to protest against jim crow?

Yes.

This confidence exuded from Dunlap and Campbell as I talked about the "how's" of the legal situation: how it would be financed, how it would be manned with lawyers, how everything would be done to minimize the use of the Danville courts as an instrument of persecution of those who both sang the "Freedom Songs" and believed what they sang.

Manpower and money were needed. I informed them that I thought the manpower situation would be easiest to solve. "Between the Committee for Legal Aid to the South (CLAS) of the Lawyers' Guild, my classmates from Howard University Law School and just plain friends in the legal profession, no one need be denied a lawyer."

"What will they be charging," Campbell asked.

"Nothing—except they ought to be fed and housed while here," I answered. "They'll merely take part of their vacation in Danville instead of in Bermuda or Bar Harbor. But what about money? Office space is needed; phones must be installed; secretaries and office equipment secured."

"Just make a list of what's needed, Snake. The Gandhi Society, Dr. King, or the Movement will somehow get what you need," Dunlap confidently added as a solution to problems already present by virtue of the one hundred arrests which had taken place.

That response wasn't encouraging. The Gandhi Society, a nonprofit organization set up by Dr. King and some of his friends to be an "attractor" of large gifts which are usually given only if the donor gets a tax deduction, had not impressed me. In nearby Lynchburg, Va., the Gandhi Society was supposed to have paid the expenses of appealing the convictions of a Negro teenager sentenced to death for an alleged rape. I was involved, along with Kunstler and Kinoy, after the trial lawyer had died. The promise of the Gandhi Society was not fulfilled. (The rape convictions were set aside and new trials ordered in September of 1964.)

It was also disquieting that somehow there was always "Dr. King" when problems were raised; he was the unseen guest in every conference; he was the giver of all solutions.

I knew that Campbell and Dunlap had not experienced what I had. Dr. King was neither omnipotent nor omnipresent.

He is a man—albeit a stirringly eloquent one.

The conference between Campbell and Dunlap and myself ended . . . on June 11, 1963.

At the High Street Church SNCC-led training sessions continued.

Later that same night, June 11, the Reverend Dr. Milton Reid, pastor of the First Baptist Church of Petersburg, Virginia, past president of the Virginia State Southern Christian Leadership Conference, and now paid functionary of the SCLC for Virginia, came to town. At the mass meeting held that night at the Bibleway Church Reid announced his mission: "To appraise the situation and to advise Dr. King of what further steps were needed." Ritualistically the mass meeting ended with "We Shall Overcome" and the folks went home to sleep and awaited the coming of a new day— of protest.

CHAPTER 9

History Nearly Repeats

If we must die, let it not be like hogs
Hunted and penned in an inglorious spot,
While round us bark the mad and hungry dogs,
Making their mock at our accursed lot.

If we must die, O let us nobly die,
So that our precious blood may not be shed
In vain; then even the monsters we defy
Shall be constrained to honor us though dead!
O kinsmen! we must meet the common foe!
Though far outnumbered let us show us brave,
And for their thousand blows deal one deathblow!
What though before us lies the open grave?
Like men we'll face the murderous, cowardly pack,
Pressed to the wall, dying, but fighting back!
　　　　　—Claude McKay, "If We Must Die"

As expected, the demonstrations which began on Wednesday, June 12, 1963, were different. Nonviolent commando squads spread the concern of Danville Negroes to a wider area of the city by inconveniencing more white persons: four restaurants on the heavily traveled major U.S. Highways were closed down with sit-ins (Howard Johnson, Charcoal House, Holiday Inn, and Staley's).

Simultaneously with the sit-ins on June 12, another

march through the downtown area and onto the steps of
City Hall was made. The Reverend Doyle Thomas, president of the local NAACP, was heading the march along
with the Reverend Lendell Chase. Thomas wanted to exert
influence in the Movement which now afforded prestige. The
price of influence was to participate in a demonstration.
These marches to the steps of City Hall seemed to be safe.
After all, Chase had led the demonstration the day before
without anyone getting arrested.

There were no arrests on June 12 of those participating
in the downtown demonstration. Chase and Thomas made
sure of this by *again* enforcing rigid compliance with every
rule suggested by the police: no traffic blocked, silent walking for the most part, marchers kept in pairs and to one
side of the sidewalk, muted singing on the steps. Yet the
police took pictures, including those of Chase and Thomas.

The calm could not last long; police hostility was merely
postponed, not ended. That suppression was evident in the
laughter of the cops when a white bystander threw a snake
in the midst of the demonstrators sitting on the steps of Danville's City Hall. "Look at the niggers scatter!" the police
commented as the demonstrators scurried away. A boy took
a cane from one of the demonstrators injured on the Night
of Infamy and killed the snake. Nothing was done to arrest
the person who had thrown it.

The following morning, Thursday, June 13, 1963, those
arrested for the sit-ins at the highway restaurants were
bailed out—including Jim Forman. More training sessions in
nonviolence were held before noon at the High Street Baptist
Church. Shortly after the noon hour, another march of
demonstrators headed for downtown. Again Reverend Chase
was leading them. Again they obeyed all the rules the Rev-

erend Chase knew about, or could think of. Leading with him was the Reverend Dr. Milton Reid.

Forman remained at the church.

Along with the CORE field secretaries, Bruce Baines and Claudia Edwards, the SNCC staffers (Cordell Reagon, Bob Zellner, Dorothy Miller Zellner, Ivanhoe Donaldson, Bernice Reagon, Daniel Foss, Avon Rollins, and Danny Lyons) conferred with Jim Forman.

Chafing between the local leadership and the more experienced, and better organized, youth could develop into a crisis. Forman wanted to avoid this. The needs of Danville were too great.

To get agreement from the CORE and SNCC workers to submerge all for unity, Forman used the logic and wealth of facts of "Negroism" that had placed him in leadership in Fayette County, Tenn.; Monroe, N.C.; and finally, at 33, at the head of SNCC in 1961. The eyes of the rights workers fixed on the rough-looking brown-skinned man as he displayed ability to think in a crisis and used his arms as eloquent accompaniments to the argument he developed to state a basic fact of the movement: "It exists for and through the local people!"

These men and women, already scarred in life by the clubs of mobs and the tongues of vindictive men, respected Forman and trusted him as few persons would ever be trusted by them. The nearly 6-foot-tall rights leaders reminded them of the *way*.

A plan was formulated. The group of rights workers dispersed and went different ways from the church.

Mayor Stinson of Danville and several other city officials had left that morning for Richmond, Virginia's capital, to confer with Governor Albertis Harrison. The Governor didn't want to send state troopers into Danville, and even more, to have a situation where state troopers were wanted. It was reported that the Governor had urged giving of token considerations—such as those which ended the Birmingham protest a few weeks before—to end the Danville matter, which was getting an ugly "press" for the State.

Armed with pictures of weapons taken from people other than demonstrators and copies of arrest records of local Danville Negroes who participated in the demonstration, Mayor Stinson sought to persuade the Governor that the worst thing for Virginia would be to negotiate with or make any concession to the "hoodlums" in Danville. The crimes listed by the Mayor were:

Larceny
Fugitive from justice
Assault
Fornication
Possession of illegal whiskey
Disorderly conduct
Concealed weapons
Drunk
Indecent exposure
Loitering
Vagrancy
Shoplifting
Violation of probation
Hit and run
Trespass
Failure to obey summons
Resisting arrest
Felonious assault
Urinating in public
Causing a juvenile to commit a misdemeanor
Breaking and entering

Discharge of firearm in city
Possession of stolen goods
Robbery
Threatening the life of another person
Being a person of ill fame
Renting a room for immoral purposes
Failure to file state income tax
Rape
Forgery
Non-support
Making false statement to secure unemployment
Engaging in a lottery
Sodomy

The Governor was informed that these crimes were attributable to 77 persons identified as demonstration participants—and that one of the demonstrators had in excess of 65 charges against him dating back to *1934*. In other words, Mayor Stinson had gone to convince the Governor that the people demonstrating in Danville against segregation were not the neat young college students wearing suits, white shirts, and ties that had conducted sit-ins during 1960; these were people who were seeking more than a cup of instant coffee and a hot dog.

And the Mayor was right.

At 5:00 P.M. on June 13, it was decided to continue the vigil on City Hall steps all night, partially as a memorial to Medgar Evers who had been slain the day before in Jackson, Miss., partially because of Danville's racial intransigence, but mostly in defiance of the crime of "being black."

Reid and Chase were not happy with this decision, but did remain.

Chase let it be known that a move would soon be made "to fill the jails." The evening paper, the Danville *Bee*,

carried news about the congratulations received by city
officials for the excellent way in which they were handling
the racial demonstrations from U.S. Senator A. Willis Robert-
son and Congressmen William M. Tuck and Watkins M.
Abbitt of Virginia.

The demonstrators' singing increased in volume about
6:00 P.M. on June 13, 1963. They had reasoned that since
the offices in the downtown area were all closed, no one
could be inconvenienced. The walls of the vacant office
buildings rocked and reverberated: "Before I'd be a slave
I'll be buried in my grave and go home to my lord and be
free." "Oh, Freedom!"

Sandwiches and cases of pop were brought to the
demonstrators. State troopers and Danville cops looked on
sullenly.

The night air became cool. The area around City Hall
was blocked off to all vehicular and pedestrian traffic. No
one was allowed to come into the area. The only thing that
could be done was to leave. Forman managed to sneak off
and make a phone call to a sweet and determined lady in
the sunset of her life, whose name must be withheld. She
quickly badgered her neighbors and secured a car to carry
the blankets hustled from other neighbors to take to the
people on the City Hall steps. A rendezvous was kept and
Forman got the blankets distributed.

At the Bibleway church the mass meeting had begun
at 8:20 P.M. At a few minutes after 11:00 P.M., Avon Rollins,
by dint of strenuous oratory, organized a group of 200 persons to join the all-night-vigil at City Hall. At the corner
of Lynn and Patton Streets, a block away from City Hall, a
column of troopers and police massed. With tear gas, clubs,
and an occasional shot, the police sent the Rollins-led group
into headlong flight. Six of them required medical treatment.

Meanwhile, Mayor Stinson and his colleagues returned from Richmond with the full cooperation and support of the Governor, who found himself persuaded to forgo *image* considerations.

Moments after the Mayor's return the persons in the vigil on the steps of City Hall were placed in position for a repeat performance of the infamy of June 10. Chief McCain and forty white-helmeted policemen rushed out the doors behind the persons on the steps. Two fire trucks uncoiled hoses and mounted up pressure. The nozzles were aimed into the midst of the group. About half the people fled in terror, including Chase and Reid, who got into a waiting car. The other fifty remained. Chief McCain raised his hand to signal the turning on of the hoses—

"Chief McCain! Chief McCain! Forman urgently cried out and signaled for the people to leave. "If you ask us to leave we'll be glad to go. Those hoses will break up all those pop bottles on these steps and it will be an awful mess to clean up in the morning." The appeal was effective.

Chief McCain looked at the cases of empty pop bottles and paused . . . "Get out of here, goddammit; I'm tired of fooling with you!"

During those precious moments the balance of the group had moved out of peril—created by the clubs and hoses, merely fifteen feet from their faces—and scattered. For a short distance police followed brandishing nightsticks.

All calmed down. Fire hoses were rolled up and stacked on the bright red pumpers. Still shaken by thoughts of what could have happened, again, in Danville, Reid and Chase politely approached Chief McCain, showing deference to his power.

"Chief McCain, would it be at all possible for us to talk with the Mayor a moment?" The Mayor was inside City

Hall. A meeting was arranged. Minutes later Reid and Chase emerged from the building with an agreement from Mayor Stinson to meet representatives of the Movement the following morning, June 14, at 10:00 A.M.

At 1:00 A.M., the battered, exhausted, and frightened victims of the two confrontations with Danville power gathered at Bibleway Church. A highly charged meeting took place. Speaker after speaker addressed the maddened and terrified gathering. Finally Reid declared: "We have won a great victory tonight."

Most of the people preferred to believe this, since under the conditions that existed it was difficult to believe that things could become worse. None involved in the Danville Movement had at that point admitted to himself the obvious: the Danville city government had decided to crush the Movement, and everyone connected with it, into a fine powder to be scattered by the wind; and then to do more, to destroy even the memory of such a protest.

At the meeting several questioned the good faith of the Mayor in having such a conference. All, however, agreed that there would be no appeasement of city officials in the choice of who would represent the Movement. Those chosen included Mrs. Beatrice Hairston, the Reverend Milton Reid, the Reverend Lawrence G. Campbell, the Reverend Lendell W. Chase, Charley Echols, the Reverend Alexander Dunlap, Julius Adams, and myself.

After Chase announced that, "at a date yet to be determined, but very soon, I am pleased to inform you that Dr. Martin Luther King and his task force from Birmingham . . . are headed for Danville," the meeting disbanded in early morning in a mood of high anticipation.

CHAPTER 10

Ambush

What I know of the mind
seems to end here;
just outside my face.
　　　—LeRoi Jones, "Epistrophe"

Like too many other Danville days in June, 1963, Friday, June 14, was pregnant with heat, hope, and opportunities for the City to display raw, naked power.

Those of us designated to represent the Danville Movement in the conference with the Mayor arrived shortly before the appointed hour. We were asked to wait in a small conference room down the hall from the Mayor's office.

The time was used to clarify the list of Movement demands and to select spokesmen to "carry the ball."

A messenger informed us that the Mayor would see us. As we approached the door to the offices, I became aware of the cluster of police near it and a small man in shirt-sleeves who had a list in his hand and who asked us our names. All went well until Julius Adams, Charles Echols, and the Reverend Campbell approached the door. "You will not be allowed to come in. The Mayor will not talk with criminals," curtly announced the little man in shirt-sleeves. Stunned, we all withdrew and went back to the conference room where we had waited earlier.

Everyone selected to represent the Movement at this

conference with the Mayor was not present. Dunlap was out of town; James Forman had responded to an urgent call to go to Cambridge, Md., where the racial protest was quite active. Of those present, only Campbell, Adams, and Echols had been arrested—at that time.

The problem was easy to describe, but not easy to decide or implement. The choices were either to take ourselves home and damn the conference because *City Hall* was trying to force us to select representatives pleasing in the Mayor's sight, or to allow those *acceptable* persons to begin a dialog.

There was the general belief that some real concession might be made because the Mayor was at last relenting to talk with representatives of the Movement while demonstrations were in progress. But even more than the belief was a need, an intensely felt need to end something that was becoming bigger than all had considered.

The principled position would have been for us all to leave. We didn't do that. We called forth our treacherous logic and southern experiences; we felt "pity" for the white folks. Someone suggested that it would be too much of a loss of face for the Mayor to meet with someone like Campbell and Adams who had helped humble the city . . . and we were interested in results. If getting results required sacrificing a "little" principle like who shall represent us, we were willing to postpone invocation of the principle.

Campbell, Adams, and Echols were put on the spot.

They too earnestly desired something that might end the impasse which the Danville Negroes seemed to be getting the worst of . . . and no one in the conference room seemed anxious, or even willing to support the principled position.

As a concession to my guilt for postponing principle and

to soothe the injury of a wrong done to the Movement and to Adams, Echols, and Campbell, I insisted that those who went into the Mayor's conference would only be messengers. "We shall make no public statements when we come out of the room. We'll confer with Campbell, Adams, and Echols, inform them of what happened, and they'll be our spokesmen with the press." It was further agreed that we would not purport to accept any offer or enter into any agreements with the Mayor, that that power of agreement and acceptance was the power that belonged solely to the leadership of the Movement.

We went into the Mayor's office.

No introductions were made—everyone seemed to know everyone else. The Mayor began. For ten minutes he made a speech touching such subjects as how "fine Danville was" and how the patience of the white community had been sorely tried by the criminal acts of Dunlap, Campbell, Adams, and several others. I winced. I hadn't come here to have the Mayor praise the Confederacy, but to get his cooperation in burying part of it.

Mrs. James C. Hughes, a well-to-do Negro undertaker who had put up tens of thousands of dollars in bail bonds to free arrested demonstrators, mentioned some aspects of Danville's racial segregation we wanted to have changed.

The Mayor denied the condition existed.

Mrs. Beatrice Hairston spoke about the unaccredited status of Langston, the Negro high school.

Mayor Stinson denied it and went on to list the magnificent things the city of Danville was doing for the Negro school children "that isn't being done for the white schools."

I felt sick. I felt ashamed. I had sacrificed principle to be a part of this—a sounding board for the republication of the official city image, a setting in which the Mayor would pose as the fair man because he sat down and talked with us. Bull—

After tugging on the sleeve of the Reverend Milton A. Reid and telling him I thought we all ought to leave, I waited a few moments. When it became apparent that he wasn't going to leave and didn't understand what was happening, I made my decision.

I left.

I stalked out of the room almost on a run. After emerging from the Mayor's office into the public corridor I was grabbed. Two detectives snatched me by the arms. One began searching me while the other asked: "Snake Doctor, are you Len Holt?"

"Why?"

"We have a warrant here for your arrest for violating the injunction of the Danville Corporation Court," he said in a twangy drawl. "Now come along quietly."

I did.

While going to police headquarters in the basement I wondered how much we knew about the minds of those who opposed us. How, for example, did we in Danville make ourselves "biblical Jobs" and the city government our "god" so that no matter what it did, we trusted it still. How long must this continue, I wondered. Every time we had one of those meetings with the Mayor something happened and we always ended up in a compromised position.

And here I was arrested for what the *Bee* described as a demonstrator: "Police said Holt had been seen at demonstrations in dungarees rather than his usual neat courtroom attire. He was arrested as he stepped from the conference rooms." An hour after being arrested, on June 14, 1963, my *first* arrest in Danville, Mr. Hester Womack bonded me out.

A few minutes after my arrest the City Council passed an anti-picketing ordinance, Ordinance 63-6.2.* The ordinance was passed shortly after 11:00 A.M. Friday, June 14, 1963. By 4:00 P.M. the next day, thirty-four demonstrators had been arrested. Each was charged with violating the newly enacted ordinance.

At the mass meeting the night of June 14 at the High Street Baptist Church, police waited outside to arrest Reid, Chase, and Zellner for violating the injunction; inside Reid spoke words of defiance and hope:

"The new ordinance is going to stir new flames in civil rights tension which will bring out new police brutality," and then indicated that Dr. Martin Luther King might come to Danville next week.

There was humor and gall in the paper the following morning, Saturday June 15, 1963.

The humor was supplied by remarks of Mayor Stinson. The reporters asked Stinson about my arrest the day before. The Mayor indicated surprise "and even at that, I still felt a little bit on the Judas side when I found out."

The galling aspect was the new ordinance, which provided a penalty of a year's confinement, quoted in the paper . . . it indicated that there was nothing that the power clique of Danville wouldn't do to crush the Movement.

Meanwhile, the truth had moved closer to the surface. The paper announced that the City Council had appointed Robert M. Gardiner, Dan River Mills' director of community relations, as the temporary Danville public relations officer.

* For full text, see pp. 232–233.

CHAPTER 11

Keep the Golden Mean

I must not assert my innocence of the allegations
he had piled up against me, for that would be
impudence.

The guilt of a slave was always and everywhere
presumed, and the innocence of the slaveholder,
or employer, was always asserted.

The word of a slave against this presumption was
treated as impudence, worthy of punishment. 'Do
you dare to contradict me, you rascal?' was the
final silencer of counter statements from the lips
of a slave.

—Frederick Douglass, *Life and Times*

Monday, June 17, 1963, was an important day for the
Danville protest because the first trial was scheduled for
those charged with violating the injunction.

There were now 105 defendants—including the Reverend Doyle Thomas. City Hall had concluded Thomas and
Chase could no longer be "praised" into a role of dividing the
Negro leadership; their conducts and public utterances had
removed all doubts.

Nothing was scheduled to begin in the Corporation
Court on June 17, 1963 until 2:30 P.M., which was fortunate;

there was a lot of scurrying to be done. Having arrived the day before from Detroit, James Lee was spending part of his vacation time as an investigator to assist the lawyers involved. He was dashing like the rest of us notifying clients that they must be on time and arranging transportation for those who lived at some distance from the downtown area and from bus lines.

Lee and I had been rushing since we had awakened early in the morning at the Campbell household and I had slapped together breakfast for the two of us amidst culinary castigations from Lee: "Man, you can't cook a lick!" or "From now on I'm going to eat out—your cooking isn't fit to slop hogs." Nevertheless, we both ate the French bacon and soft scrambled eggs.

We had to ourselves the 3-room bungalow belonging to the Reverend Campbell and his wife; the flow of crank calls and bomb threats had caused Mrs. Campbell to send her children out of town and to abandon the house.

Emotionally she was still tense from the beating inflicted on her on June 10 as one of the fifty persons who went to the jail to pray. "Almost every night I'm forced to relive it," she told us.

The white 1962 Renault was parked hurriedly in what was soon to become its favorite resting place: the entrance on South Main Street of the office of Harvey and Wood.

Jim and I were pleased to see that Harry I. Wood, the legal theoretician of the firm, was there and could let us in. Without formal notice or request, and primarily because of the generosity of Harry Wood and Miss Ruth Harvey, the Movement lawyers had commandeered the facilities of the law office. Harry had been up for hours checking the motions that had been prepared and mimeographed the day before.

Having one of the best equipped law libraries in Danville and a love of books, Harry was in an excellent position to do a meticulous job.

On the day before, Sunday, June 16, when there had been a conference on the pending injunction cases attended by the five Danville Negro lawyers, Sam W. Tucker, Jim Lee, and myself, Harry's personality exuded an inspiring mirth that had made our arduous jobs of drafting motions, looking at law books, and deciding the "who's" and "how's" and "when's" easier.

Today was different.

Harry wasn't smiling. His well-developed body, which had garnered him fame in football, track, and basketball at Howard University, was taut as if there were but a few seconds left to play in the final quarter and the Howard U. *Bisons* were two points behind on their opponents 16-yard line. The greeting was short:

"Hi Len, Jim. Your motions are over there," he said pointing a finger attached to an arm of the size usually found on the longshoremen on Wide Street in Norfolk where I lived.

Jim began calling the people who had either been by, or phoned earlier to get me to represent them before Judge Aiken. I began counting, signing and arranging the motions into folders: there were thirty-four of them including one marked "Me"—for I too was a defendant before the Corporation Court. The motions were checked, filed and signed and I felt better. I took time then to give a gentle pat to "Goldie," an ancient, chubby, cocker spaniel whose name reflected his color.

At that point of the day of June 17, 1963, there were many serious concerns, all of which defied resolution except by waiting: Who would be tried first, and would briefs be required by Judge Aiken in support of our motions? How much time would be allowed? Would the lawyers promised by Ernie Goodman arrive in time? Would there be jury trials? Could the bonds be kept low on appeal? How many more would be arrested before . . . before the protest would end in our favor? Was Martin Luther King coming—and what could he do after he got in Danville? Why was the FBI so slow in bringing prosecutions against the Danville authorities for the bludgeonings of the demonstrators on June 10th? And what about the people without lawyers— what will happen to them?

What about the people?

There were, on that day, 105 persons charged with violating the injunction of the Danville Corporation Court (a figure that would grow to 370 before the summer ended). I represented 36 of them; Andrew C. Muse about five; Harry Wood and his wife fifteen; Jerry Williams approximately ten. There were some thirty-nine without counsel and unless they called here or one of the other offices within the next few hours and asked for a lawyer to represent them they might be seriously denied some right because of unfamiliarity with procedures and the fright of appearing alone before a judge.

On this matter the lawyers were helpless . . . because this was Virginia.

As the morning sun climbed toward the highest part of the sky on June 17, 1963, and the temperature rose with it, I began sweating, my skin became oily. Jim Lee was still calling clients. The air was interlaced with the pine odor of dog soap used to bathe Goldie, who had stretched out on the floor near my feet; his tongue hung haphazardly out of the side of his mouth and he panted at a furious rate because the temperature was approaching the 90's.

Only two more hours, or so, to wait for the trial or "something" to begin before Judge Archibald M. Aiken. Jim Lee had stopped phoning.

To relax I turned my attention to the paper, but it aroused instead of relaxed; featured on the front page was a story about the civil rights infighting:

NAACP Official Assails CORE, Other Groups

Alexandria, Va. (AP)—Roy Wilkins, executive secretary of the National Association for the Advancement of Colored People, charged Sunday that other groups "furnished the noise" while the NAACP "pays the bills" in such racial hotspots as Jackson, Miss.

Wilkins criticized the Congress of Racial Equality (CORE), the Student Non-violent Coordinating Committee and the Southern Christian Leadership Conference headed by Dr. Martin Luther King.

I put the paper down.

About that time, through the front door came several wonderful surprises. The "Guild," CLAS, had come through with help. There, frightened and anxious because it was their first trip to a racial protest center, were Nathan Conyers (Detroit trial attorney) and Dean Robb (half of the best personal injury lawyer team in the midwest). And then another surprise came in, William M. Kunstler of the "KKK" —a law firm whose three senior partners all have the last initial of "K": Kunstler, Kunstler and Kinoy.

Bill Kunstler is tall, angular, graceful, and reminds one of how Lincoln must have looked at the age of forty or so. By then Jerry Williams, Andrew Muse, George Woody, and Ruth Harvey had come into the office and there was bedlam as the cacophony of boisterous greetings, back-slapping, hugs and hollers commenced, a common event when members of that small club of civil rights lawyers see each other after an absence. A short gray-haired lady waiting to see Ruth about an estate seemed surprised at the intensity of the greetings:

"Seems like a family reunion, Ruth."

"It is!"

All the lawyers at that point were one. And then Kunstler spoke about utilization of the *Kunstler Statute*, a nickname given to Title 28, Section 1443 of the United States Code. This federal statute, enacted as part of the *Reconstruction Legislation*, permits the removal, or transfer, of criminal or civil cases brought in a state court to the nearest United States District Court. For a hundred years the statute remained in the United States Code, neatly tucked away and dormant until William Higgs, an ex-Mississippi lawyer, called it to Kunstler's attention while Kunstler was in Jackson, Miss., defending some of the Freedom Riders. Ever since, Kunstler had been invoking the statute whenever he was called in to give assistance in a racial protest.

We were no longer one, a group. We became fractions. In one unit were the five Danville Negro lawyers headed by Ruth Harvey; they were NAACP lawyers. They would represent those persons who had retained them. Privately, cooperation in every way would be the rule. Publicly things would be separate. They were NAACP lawyers and the leaders of the Danville Movement had rejected the NAACP offer. This meant that there would be no joint filing of motions or other papers. Their position was both understandable and justified. In the other group were all the rest of us.

Kunstler pressed the filing of a removal for their clients asserting that they could invoke the *Statute* in a separate petition. They didn't have to join in my petition.

Kunstler's assumption that I would have no objection to filing under his statute irked just a little because there had been no discussion of the matter, but I said nothing.

One of the local Danville lawyers called Jack Greenberg of the NAACP Legal Defense Fund in New York to get his ideas on employing the *Statute*. The message relayed indicated that Greenberg had flatly said "No," that it was a crazy legal technique that should never be used because it was just a waste of good time, that it constituted almost a "playing with the courts."

"What about you, Snake?" Kunstler asked in a tone which reflected his discouragement with the position taken by Greenberg.

"Yeah, Bill Kunstler. Me an' you."

Within a blink, Kunstler withdrew from his brief case a sample removal petition "that he just happened to have on him." Nathan Conyers and Kunstler went to the secretary, "Lawyer Mac," Miss A. D. McCain, and began showing her what they wanted typed on a stencil to be run quickly. "Please hurry. This must be filed in the U.S. District Court here in Danville before we go to Corporation Court. Leave the front page blank. Start on page two. We'll give you a list of names to put on the front page in a moment," Kunstler told "Lawyer Mac." Nathan Conyers remained with her to answer questions she might have about the petition so that it wouldn't be necessary for her to walk to the back room. Conyers performed another function just as important.

He answered the busy phone that would have robbed "Lawyer Mac" of precious time.

In the back office, simultaneously, Dean Robb helped me compile a list of names of the clients I represented. This was most important. Any name not included on the petition would not be removed from the state court.

Jim Lee moved toward the duplicating machine and prepared it for the "hot run." Harry Wood helped momentarily and then called Jerry Williams and the others over to his desk where last minute details were again gone over. It was decided that I would be permitted to proceed first in the Corporation Court because I was filing a removal of the cases from the Corporation Court to Danville's United States District Court.

On finishing the compiling of names for the first sheet of the petition Kunstler, Dean Robb, and I talked about the removal statute while waiting for the mechanical job of typing and duplicating to be finished: Lawyer Mac's fingers scampered across the keyboard; the bell signaling the end of a line was ringing at rapid intervals.

We talked. I frankly told Kunstler I didn't think much of removing the cases to federal court. "For once in our lives, Jack Greenberg and I are in agreement," I informed Bill Kunstler and Dean Robb. "But I'm going along because I don't see how my clients can lose anything. I've got the feeling that it might at least buy them—us—time and that's what we need a whole lot of now. All this cooperation and funds for setting up an office, and things like that, are taking a long time to come from SCLC and the Gandhi Society."

"That doesn't seem to be a problem," Bill said. "You seem to be functioning well out of this setting."

"But that's it. They shouldn't let us in this door. I'm a tenant in here by sufferance. As a professional courtesy and because of the concern of Harry and Ruth for the Movement, we are functioning. The Movement has made no arrangements as of this date with Harry for all this disruption you see," I told Bill and Dean.

Sensing a little bitterness in my voice, Dean Robb changed the subject. "Gee, Snake Doctor. You've got to admit that the petition for removal that Kunstler presented is simple and routine. Three little ol' pages," said in a midwestern drawl that sounded much like the speech of a popular cowboy actor. I remembered then that Dean is from a little "cracker" town in southern Illinois that's a replica of Hattiesburg, Miss., in more unpleasant ways than one.

The removal petition was simple. And it was fast. Kunstler explained how it became effective when but three things were done: it's filed with the Clerk of the U.S. District Court; a copy is served on the Clerk of the Danville Corporation Court; and a copy is given to the Commonwealth Attorney (who serves as the prosecutor of the cases). The beautiful thing was that anyone can serve the papers on the Clerk and the Prosecutor. This was a help to speed. In Danville there was no federal marshal. The nearest one was forty miles away, near Martinsville, and it might take a day before you could get him to come and serve papers.

The petition with thirty-six names was duplicated and all copies signed. Transportation was arranged for the lawyers in two cars. It was 2:10 P.M. Then a crisis arose.

It took $15.00 to file the removal petition.

We had to "church-up" the money . . . advance it to our clients until they paid us back—a joke in Movements. Among the ten of us one five dollar bill and ten singles were collected. Off to Corporation Court we went for a legal proceeding with, as someone described it, "the courage of attorney Melvin Belli."

Because such unity of opposition had developed in the Negro community by June 17, 1963, to the tactics and objectives of those who ran *City Hall* there wasn't a Negro around willing to accept the title of being "reliable" or "responsible" or "upright" or "intelligent" from *City Hall.*

This created a problem for those on the other side of the tracks.

Mayor Stinson had recently appointed a *Mayor's Advisory Committee.* It was the ostensible function of this white three-man committee to study and advise proper solution of the City's racial matters. Its real function was to be a front, a nothingness, which the public relations man, Richard M. Gardiner (loaned to Danville by the Dan River Mills to improve the sordid image of the City) could utilize in press releases as proof, "We love our Negroes and are working to help them." Its second function was to encourage the historical, and deep, leadership split among Negroes by meeting with, and giving status thereby to, "Negro leaders" who shunned involvement in racial protest. (The same technique was used in Harlem in 1964.)

The Mayor's Advisory Committee failed—understandably so.

It was lily white.

It was headed by William J. Erwin, President of Dan River Mills.

It could confer no status in June of 1963 that any Danville Negro citizen wanted. So a strange thing happened. On June 17, before the hour set for the trials of the 105 persons then charged with the violation of the Corporation Court injunction, contempt, and while Jim Lee, Harry Wood, and I were worrying and preparing for those trials, and rejoicing that Dean Robb and Nat Conyers had arrived from Detroit to join the legal team . . . the Mayor's Advisory Committee was meeting.

In that meeting were Julius Adams, the Reverend Alexander I. Dunlap, the Reverend Lawrence G. Campbell, the Reverend L. W. Chase, the Reverend C. R. McCreary, and the Reverend J. H. Jones—all proud black men. Only McCreary and Jones had not openly identified themselves previously with the Movement. Adams, Dunlap, and Campbell were under indictment under the "John Brown" statute. The image of Danville to the outside world was so sordid —and perhaps, brutal—that the Mayor's Advisory Committee was willing to meet with the Movement leaders for the sake of news releases.

And the Movement demands (not requests, but demands) were presented, four of them:

1. All charges against demonstrators dropped.

2. Establishment of a fair employment policy in city jobs beginning with the hiring of at least ten Negro policemen, one stenographer, and two clerks.

3. Desegregation within thirty days of all hotels, motels, and restaurants.

4. Establishment of a biracial committee to set a timetable for the desegregation of all schools; the all-white, 315-bed, Memorial Hospital; and official boards of the city government.

On the latter point the Movement leaders offered an alternative of appointment of a Negro to the Mayor's all-white Advisory Committee. In either event, the Movement leaders indicated, the person selected must be acceptable to them. Further demonstrations were temporarily suspended until the Mayor's Advisory Committee could meet again.

At 2:26 P.M., June 17, 1963, the two cars drove into the little service station parking lot across from the 4-story, mute gray City Hall where somewhere on the fourth floor in an area with an elevated desk called "the bench" there would sit a judge, Judge Archibald M. Aiken. In that courtroom on that day we were to confront the power of Virginia and Danville and be dispensed justice.

For the length of the long sidewalk near the basement entrance to City Hall people were standing, black people. They stood in silence and with straight faces. A few smiled when they saw their lawyers. There were at least two hundred of them, some there because they were defendants, others there because they cared. All of them looked at the eight lawyers as they strode across the street, but they did not push, move, or otherwise gain any advantage over the others waiting to get into the building. A way was made for the lawyers—to enter the basement door, the only one of the five entrances to the building now open. At the other four doors there were locks and guards as if there were some dangerous animals around who had indicated an imminent desire to break into the building and devour the people inside. From the revelations of the past few days in Danville it was most probable that the situation was vice-versa.

Four guards were at the door of the basement, each with gun and club. Dean Robb and William Kunstler were admitted without question; they are white. The rest of us were stopped.

"What ya want in here, what's ya business?"

"We're lawyers. We're going upstairs to see that these people have some constitutional rights," Ruth told him in a voice that revealed indignation.

Inside the corridor on the basement floor were policemen: state troopers, city cops in uniform, city cops not in uniform. With feet at a wide stance and some fingering the top of their holstered guns, they blocked passage beyond the two elevators which sat at the center of the long corridor. The two elevator doors were opened; there were white men with guns, guards, running them in place of the usual two Negro ladies. To the right of the elevator the steps were barred; the only way up or down was by way of the guarded elevators which opened on each floor to reveal more cops guarding each exit: Though there were hundreds of people in the box-like building there was little noise, little to indicate that so many were present because of the funeral parlor silence.

On the top floor, the fourth floor, we got off the elevator and went to our right to the foyer of the Corporation Court. We were stopped.

"What are you? Are you lawyers, defendants, witnesses or what?" asked the tallest of the three policemen at the outer door of the foyer.

"Lawyers," we all answered when the question was put to us. We then stepped inside. Bill Kunstler and Dean Robb proceeded ahead without difficulty and moved into the courtroom. They are white. The rest of us were stopped and searched—Nathan Conyers, Harry Wood, Andrew Muse, George Woody, Jerry Williams, and myself. We're black. The muscular cop searching me had a grin on his face. As his stubby, strong fingers worked their way down from my shoulders, in between my arms and on the outside and inside of my legs he would dig a thumb into my flesh and stare at my face to see the reaction. With a grimace, I tried to conceal the pain and the anger and did a good job until I looked to my left.

There was Ruth Harvey. She was being searched. "Oh, these bastards, these mammy-jammers," I said to myself in shame for my own helplessness and the helplessness of all of us who could do nothing to stop any indignity—no matter how gross or raw, that Danville might think of. Here in broad daylight, in front of national newsmen, we were being brutalized and prevented from living like men. But this was a courtroom where justice was going to be dispensed.

Dean Robb and Bill were livid with anger. Every black face was grimmer than before. It wouldn't have taken much for a soul, whose cup of tolerance had overflowed, to have given a signal or cry—we would have all understood it— and there to cover our shame and indignation of being robbed of manhood, mauled in the search like animals and being forced to see women treated likewise, a battle would have been fought in which some of us might have died in a way Danville and Virginia had never let us live: like men.

That signal or cry was never given. Our survival system of accommodating, perpetual accommodating, maintained control. I pass no judgment on this matter except to relate it as I felt it, saw it, and the confirmation from later conversations that others shared these emotions and thoughts.

The courtroom itself is odd. It is doubtful that there is another like it anywhere. There is one center aisle about eight feet wide with solemn, dark-colored benches for spectators running off both sides of that aisle. Only from the center aisle can entrance be gained to those benches. The other ends of them are closed by railings that run between columns that support the high ceiling of the courtroom, which is also the roof of the building. A great deal of light comes into the courtroom from windows strategically placed near the ceiling which encourages consciousness of the position of the sun, hence, the passage of time. The dimensions of the courtroom are about 60 by 130 feet, and there are aisles which form a circular corridor around the judge's bench, the counsel tables arranged in the form of a horseshoe, and the spectator's benches.

On the left passageway facing directly into the open courtroom are several rooms, two of which are the chambers of Judge Aiken. On the right corridor circling the arrangement are some more rooms. Two of them have the added convenience of putting the juror's mind at ease by having four toilets each with a label: one pair is labeled "Men"; the other, "Ladies." There are other designations above the stalls containing commodes which provide a "freedom of choice": "Colored" and "White."

And the white leaders of Danville wouldn't have it any other way.

Just as the entire building was crowded with police, so was the courtroom. State troopers were in the courtroom, fifteen of them, adorned in steel gray uniforms, and bearing clubs and black 38-caliber pistols with 6-inch barrels (horse guns). "Danville's finest," 25 of them, were spread out over this chamber of justice, weaponized similar to that of the state troopers except for the clubs. In place of clubs there were blackjacks that were 8 inches long, a half-inch thick, black in color and flat so they fit into pockets with ease and don't make sitting uncomfortable. Added to these were a baker's dozen detectives and deputy City Sergeants (bailiffs), including one named Luke Reynolds who wore a monstrous magnum (magnums are pistols that shoot rifle-size bullets that can pierce engine blocks).

The City Sergeant rapped on the gavel and all in the courtroom stood while Judge Aiken entered and took his place on the bench. Then began the roll call of defendants by the Clerk of the Corporation Court, T. Tucker. One hundred and five names were called; one hundred names answered. Bruce Baines of CORE and several others were still in jail and had not been brought into the courtroom.

Kunstler, Robb and Conyers, who were from out-of-state, were introduced to the Court and permission was asked for them to associate on the cases. Dean Robb and

Nat Conyers, who had been forewarned, brought with them proof of being members of the Michigan Bar. They were permitted to associate. Kunstler, having brought no credentials, was not, although he was permitted to sit at counsel table. This procedure of bringing certificates is out of the ordinary. Customarily when a member of a local bar introduces another attorney to the Court that ends it. The vouchsafement of the local attorney is usually the only proof required that the person being introduced is an attorney. (Later, certificates of bar memberships weren't enough; the clerk, T. Tucker, began calling to secretaries of bar associations of the out-of-town lawyer's home state.)

The insistence on credentials was not the only galling ruling of that afternoon.

The petitions to remove the cases of thirty-four persons were served on the Commonwealth Attorney, Eugene Link, and the Clerk, T. Tucker. I then turned to Judge Aiken and asked that the thirty-four persons named in the petition removing their cases to the U.S. District Court for the Western District of Virginia be excused.

"No. We're going to try these cases," was the reply. I was at that point naive enough to believe that if Commonwealth Attorney Link just took a little time to read the petition, and read the book we offered containing the *Statute* in the United States Code, that Link would advise Judge Aiken that the Corporation Court could not proceed. I was wrong. Again I spoke to Judge Aiken:

"Your Honor, it would have the effect . . . it is not discretionary, sir, of removing these thirty-four cases to federal court. They are removed. They are now federal cases. This court is without power to act against the thirty-four persons listed in the petition."

"Let's proceed with the cases," Judge Aiken responded.

It was then that motions were filed attacking the constitutionality of the Danville Corporation Court injunction. To this we were told that the constitutionality of the injunction was not in issue. "We are here to find out whether these people have violated the injunction," Judge Aiken replied.

Then thirty-four motions asking for bills of particulars were filed. This was needed because the injunction had a dozen provisions which purported to set out different wrongful acts. We didn't think it fair to force people to come into court on the day of trial and have to guess what "wrongful acts" they have supposedly committed.

The motions were denied.

A continuance was asked for all thirty-four cases because, "in light of His Honor's ruling we would have to make additional preparation."

"Motion denied."

We asked for indication as to when individual persons would be tried so that everybody wouldn't have to come to court every day and just sit.

"Denied."

Objection was noted to the searching prodecure and to the police-dominated atmosphere as inimical to a due process trial; the motion was not granted.

Judge Aiken then spoke to the other attorneys, the Danville Negro attorneys: "Was Mr. Holt making motions for your clients, too?"

"No, your Honor. Our defenses are separate. We think those motions are good, your Honor, but we are filing our own," Jerry Williams hastily informed the court as he passed over mimeographed motions identical with the ones I had filed. I had copied the motion from him.

The responses to Jerry Williams' motions were identical to those I made: denied.

This hearing before Judge Aiken in the Danville Corporation Court on June 17, 1963, was the first judicial confrontation had by those charged with violating the injunction, contempt, issued by Aiken eleven days before. The only thing the 105 persons knew was that they were supposed to have violated that injunction; the little mimeographed form given to them gave that information.

No one knew what, how, when, or where they were supposed to have violated it. Nor did they know which one of its more than a dozen provisions they had supposedly violated. This is not unusual at an initial confrontation with the court, such as this confrontation was. The proper procedure to be followed is for the court or the prosecution to inform the person accused of the specifics and then allow the accused to have time in which to prepare a defense based on the specific information or to take other steps, such as a plea of guilty.

For example, a person, let's call him John Smith, is arrested on Main Street Thursday afternoon while doing nothing more than peacefully gazing into a store window containing expensive diamond bracelets. The following morning, Friday, he is brought before the judge, charged with disorderly conduct. Smith's lawyer, a gentleman by the name of E. A. Dawley, asks for specifics by way of a bill of *particulars*. The court then informs Smith and his attorney that the disorderly conduct consisted of a fist fight of serious consequences which occurred Monday afternoon in the office of a local stockbroker.

With this specific information Smith is now able to defend himself. A continuance is granted, the case is set for trial at a later day, and Smith's lawyer busies himself securing witnesses to show that on the Monday when the fight was supposed to have taken place, his client had been thousands of miles away in Las Vegas receiving congratulations for having cut the margin of the Negro vote for Kennedy in New York.

Specifics are essential when one is charged with an offense such as these 105 persons were in Danville.

It was also important that specific dates for the trial of each of the 105 persons be given. We wanted to avoid the hardships that resulted for the defendants when each one had to appear every day and sit all day while other persons were being tried. Many of the persons charged with contempt and violation of the injunction were mothers with small children who had to be cared for; others were students enrolled in summer school, still others were employed persons who faced loss of jobs providing meager incomes with which they enabled their families to exist.

For the lawyers defending the persons in court that morning, a public trial was more than a mere Constitutional Right. Our experiences had taught us that public trials aid defendants. Often, as in Danville, policemen lie. When the lying is done in a public trial it is not uncommon for members of the public to contact defense lawyers at one of the recesses of the trial and provide information to the defense lawyer which will enable him to produce proof of lying or perjury on the part of prosecution witnesses.

On June 17, 1963, the accused persons were without *particulars,* a specific date for a trial, and without the advantages of the public scrutiny of the testimony of prosecution witnesses.

After a few more preliminary remarks between the Court and counsel, the Commonwealth Attorney announced he was going to proceed by trying Ezell Barksdale. Barksdale was one who had asked me to represent him. I noted that he was a seventeen-year-old high school senior.

A motion was made to dismiss the proceedings because Barksdale was a juvenile. Under Virginia law all persons seventeen or under are juveniles, and before a Corporation Court can proceed against them criminally there has to be a hearing in juvenile court and a recommendation that the juvenile be treated as an adult.

"Motion denied."

The motion was made for Barksdale's right to a public trial (the public had been denied entrance) and for a jury trial.

"Motions denied."

The City then put on evidence that there was an injunction, and that Ezell Barksdale had participated in the late morning, early afternoon demonstration on June 10. The examination of the prosecutor was lengthy and detailed. The cross-examinations were short, we had no desire to remind them of essential facts like "notice" which had not been proven.

City Manager C. Edward Temple, the first witness for the prosecution, had testified that in a demonstration which had occurred a week before, on June 11, he had "assigned as many policemen as possible to protect this *mob*," referring to those demonstrating.

With all the sarcasm that could be marshaled, on cross-examination Temple was asked,

"From whom?"

"Other elements in the community who might not agree with what they were doing," was the reply.

"What were the demonstrators doing?" he was asked.

"What they were fighting for, I'm not qualified to say. I think it had to do with their chant, 'We want freedom!' But what they meant by that I don't know."

Hope surged in bosoms that Temple would be taught his needed lesson—soon.

I was cocky.

In the short period that I had discussed the statute for removing cases from a state court to federal court and from a reading of the statute—all under the tutelage of Bill Kunstler—I knew that 28 U.S.C. 1443 was final and absolute until a federal judge sent the cases back to the state court. And that hadn't been done. Knowledge made me cocky, and as Nat, Dean, and Bill expressed concern about a question asked by the prosecutor of a witness I shushed them: "Cool it, Baby." From my point of view there was only a problem of keeping bail for Barksdale at the $500 rate he was now out on, or not getting it much higher.

At the conclusion of all testimony on June 17, 1963, all motions made earlier were renewed. As before, they were "denied." In view of what the court's conclusion would be, no further statements were made until the adjudication of guilt and sentencing.

Ezell Barksdale stood before the Judge's bench. "I sentence you to serve ninety days, half of which I will suspend on condition of your good behavior for a period of two years, and that you pay a fine of $25.00."

A motion was made that the sentence be delayed in enforcement pending appeal (a stay of execution) and the present $500 bond continued.

A stay of execution, a delay in enforcing order sending Barksdale to jail, and bail were important to allow for the exoneration of Barksdale. It was June 17, 1963, summer.

The court to which an appeal of the Danville conviction had to be taken, the Virginia Supreme Court of Appeals, was on vacation. Barksdale had a 45-day sentence. Before the Virginia Supreme Court of Appeals convened in the fall, Barksdale would have served the forty-five days. Furthermore, more often than not, two years can pass from the date of conviction in a trial court and a decision by the Virginia Supreme Court of Appeals asserting that the conviction in the trial court was wrong.

Judge Aiken picked up a typed memorandum and began to read:

. . . the community is confronted, and has been confronted for some days, with a race riot. There is violence . . . constantly prevailing day and night that could erupt with disastrous results at any moment. . . . This injunction was issued by me on June 6 in an effort to suppress such violence . . . to grant such a suspension or stay would prolong indefinitely violations of the injunction and render it worthless. . . . It is the duty of this Court to bring this riot and insurrection to a peaceful termination as quickly as possible . . .

We were stunned—lawyers, demonstrators, and out-of-town newsmen. The denial of a stay of execution and bail meant absolute jail for every one of the demonstrators. Before an appeal could be docketed in the Virginia Supreme Court and a decision rendered, the sentence would have been served. Murmurs rose among the Negro demonstrators, all ninety-nine who had been forced to remain for this trial. They knew that what had happened to Barksdale would happen to them; the thought wasn't comforting. I was dumbfounded. I've been in hundreds of southern courts and seen a lot done in the name of "justice." None of those experiences had prepared me for this day, and this event.

The other lawyers were similarly thunderstruck, except one.

"Get it in the record. Get it in the record," Nat Conyers whispered frantically as in one motion he jerked my head down to him. At first I was perplexed; get "what" in the record . . . then it *hit* me.

"Your Honor, pardon me. But as you were reading from what appears to be a 3-page typewritten memorandum within seconds of my motion to stay execution of the sentence, I'm not certain that I heard everything you said clearly. Does the court have an extra copy of the typed statement just read so that I might read it, please?"

It was in the record. The court reporter taking down the testimony had just included my request. At a day soon to come it would be helpful to show strong evidence that the judge might have predetermined the guilt of the accused before trial and had prepared a typewritten memorandum containing a speech as to why there would be no bail pending appeal.

All of the remaining persons charged were ordered back to the Corporation Court the next morning, June 18, 1964, knowing not which one of us would be tried and jailed without bail next.

That day was an experience. It did for the Movement lawyers what they could not have done on their own: resolve petty differences arising out of organizational loyalty. Everyone was mad. The heat of that madness welded together a team that was to function well in the weeks that followed.

On the way out of the police-cluttered building, Lawyer George Woody spoke: "Let's go to work." And go to work we did. That night, June 17, 1963, was to be the first of many all-night sessions of lawyers working for the Danville Movement. But first Bill Kunstler had to be taken to the airport for a return to New York. As he departed, he left a commitment to handle such appellate work as we might call on him to perform, even if the promised pay didn't come from either the Gandhi Society or SCLC. This was a big help because there just weren't legal library facilities for research in Danville. I ducked out of being a part of the farewell committee; there was another duty to be performed, reassuring the people.

On the way out of City Hall there were nearly inaudible whispers passed back and forth among the Negroes: "Go to the church" or "High Street." And to the High Street Baptist Church the persons charged with violating the injunction went along with others: their friends, some relatives and the just plain curious from the Negro community. The events witnessed in the courtroom were not easy to understand and many wondered how it all happened, but they had seen a solemn-faced Ezell Barksdale led off to jail, they understood this, and they didn't like it. "All those lawyers there and they couldn't stop it," was written in the face of some. There was a need for assurance, understanding or anything that would wash away those looks of helplessness.

There was a short prayer by a minister, which began in submissive supplication for care and protection by "You, Almighty God," and moved into tones of disgust as the prayer admitted to God, and those in the Sunday School auditorium of High Street, "I cain't ask you to bless those henchmen of the devil who sit in high places in our city cause it ain't in my heart," then concluded with black defiance: "We ain't gonna let Judge Aiken turn us around! We just ain't!"

Then I spoke. In plain terms it was explained how things had developed, why the lawyers had done what they did in the way they did it. "Without qualification," they were told, "what you saw today is wrong, legally and morally. And don't ever forget that just like there is a God in heaven there are also people here on this earth who will carry out his will." The black faces seemed to have more hope as my voice rang with certainty . . . the kind a speaker uses to convince himself as much as those to whom he is speaking. "Don't ever forget that there are federal courts and that there is a thing called the Constitution and that Virginia—whether it likes it or not—is still part of the United States."

"Tell it!" someone shouted.

"What has been done here today will be set aside swiftly when we once get the matter before a fair judge. And tomorrow while we are in Danville some of those eight lawyers which you saw in the courtroom today won't be there. They'll be in Charlottesville. They'll be before Judge Michie of the federal court. They'll present the ugly facts of today and ask him, *'Are you the fair judge we've been looking for?'* All attention was focused on me. I was "preaching."

"And you know what he's gonna say! Do you know what ol' Judge Michie is gonna say?"

"Freedom!" Cordell Reagon screamed in reply. We all felt better. Then the conversation with the gathering of 200 became less emotional. They were cautioned about being punctual, not responding to the provocation of the rough handling during the search, and making sure that there was nothing on them when they went to court that they weren't willing to share with Judge Aiken. They understood and laughed. And then became serious again. I too was a defendant, and this shouldn't be forgotten.

The power structure of Danville had developed a certain hatred of the "Snake Doctor." This hatred began in August of 1962, a year before the beginning of the Danville Protest, when I had filed the *Danville Omnibus Integration Suit* for the Movement leaders (Julius Adams, and the Reverends Dunlap, Campbell, and Chase) in the Danville Federal court. This suit sought to force the integration of everything "public" in Danville.

On June 13, 1963, it was known to *City Hall* that I had undertaken direction of the legal affairs of the Danville Movement and the recruiting of northern lawyers to insure that nobody would be denied his right to legal counsel.

On the afternoon of June 13, 1963, I had been seen in the area of the Municipal Building observing the demonstration being conducted there. The decision had been made to arrest me. This decision was implemented as I left the conference in Mayor Stinson's office the morning of June 14, 1963.

The logic was easily understood: The folks would not continue the protest unless they had legal assistance when arrested. I was directing and marshaling that legal assistance. An arrest of the "Snake Doctor" could either eliminate aid or make it controllable.

Though arrested, and even convicted of contempt, I could still serve because neither arrest nor conviction amounted to disbarment. My service would only end if after conviction I were flung in jail without bail as Ezell Barksdale had been hours before on June 17, 1963. I could defend no one while behind bars. It was being out of jail that gave *City Hall* its greatest possibility of control.

When a lawyer defends other persons before a judge who is also destined to pass upon the innocence of the lawyer himself, there's pressure on the lawyer to curry favor and ingratiate himself with that judge. This ingratiating is done by doing nothing to displease the judge who may soon sentence the lawyer. By arresting me on June 14, 1963, *City Hall* had hoped for neutralization at the price of detriment to my clients.

When a lawyer is charged with a crime and is defending clients before a judge who will preside over the lawyer's trial, one of two steps should be taken: the lawyer should either withdraw as counsel or be tried before his clients are tried. Either step removes self-preservation as a factor in the trial equation.

I did neither.

Instead I over-compensated in the other direction. Unconsciously, to prove to myself that I was as much of a *true believer* as my partner Joe Jordan, the level and degree of my advocacy on behalf of my clients was intensified into a holy war. No concessions, not even reasonable ones, were made. Extra efforts and drive, drive, drive, resulted in an effort to teach *City Hall* "bloody instructions." I needed to know that I could be more than I was . . . that the "Snake Doctor" would not sell his principles for the porridge of personal escape. It appears that I succeeded.

One week later after the first arrest on June 14, I was to be indicted under the John Brown law with ten other persons.

I looked into the inspiring faces of the students, ministers, mothers, children, and *freedom-starved* people and gave suggestions as to what they must do if the next day, or the next, they found themselves without legal help because I had been put in jail. Those gathered seemed to understand. And then it happened, one of those events that gives reason to the meaning of all the protests I had assisted or engaged in from Tallahassee to New York—a hand went up and started waving for permission to ask a question. It was a boy of about 12. I recognized him.

"Should we sing?" he asked.

"If you want to sing, sing. We're all going to jail anyway; we might as well go singing as any other way." The circle was then formed and "We Shall Overcome" was sung with more feeling and meaning than I've heard before. Look out, Danville.

CHAPTER 12

Castration

Whither?
North is greed and South is blood;
within, the coward, and without the liar.
Whither? To Death?
    —W. E. B. Du Bois, *Soul of the Republic*

Quick sandwiches had been eaten, and Jerry Williams, Andrew Muse, George Woody, Ruth Harvey, and Harry Wood had been to their respective law offices and checked phone messages and urgent mail left by their secretaries. By 6:00 P.M. on June 17, 1963, they were all gathered at the office of Harvey and Wood on South Main Street, stripped of ties, some stripped of shoes, stripped of reservations—and mad. Work assignments were handed out. Dean Robb and Harry Wood were to draw up a complaint to be filed in the morning attacking the Danville Picketing ordinance. Nathan Conyers and Ruth Harvey were to prepare the trial brief, secure a court reporter, and handle the trials of six persons charged with trespass in the Municipal Court in the morning for a restaurant sit-in and also cover the matters that might occur in the Juvenile Court with parents of demonstrators arrested in a move to force their children not to demonstrate. George Woody and Andrew Muse were carrying out the tasks of interviewing the flood of people

coming into the office asking for representation, getting retainer forms signed, arranging transportation for the lawyers going to Charlottesville in the morning with such suits
and complaints as were ready by the morning, while at
the same time perfecting an appeal to the Virginia State
Supreme Court for Barksdale on the matter of bail until it
could be heard on the merits.

Jerry Williams and I worked on drafting another removal petition. Under this one we would remove from the
Corporation Court to the federal court all of the remaining
cases of those charged with violation of the state court
injunction. Persons who had been lawyer-less this morning
had all finally contacted one of us to represent them. All
of these persons were placed on the same petition regardless
of which lawyer they had asked to represent them in court.
The second petition contained a categorical listing of all
the denials of due process arising out of the trial earlier in
the day. Jerry Williams made no mention of the phone call
to Jack Greenberg and his opposition to removing the cases
to federal court, nor did I, but Jerry did smile. That smile
conveyed a lot of meaning. That smile said "Jack Greenberg is in New York and I'm here and I know more about
what Danville needs than he does."

"Lawyer Mac" and Mrs. Magnolia Jefferys were beating
a steady machine-gun rhythm on their typewriters as the
lawyers flooded them with scribbled pieces of paper containing drafts of complaints, affidavits, retainer forms, trial
briefs, motions, covering letters, points and authorities, and
supporting memoranda, and a dozen other things.

Shortly the hand-cranked mimeographed machine, affectionately named "Lumumba," was clicking and clacking
as it gulped reams of paper to spew them forth with messages of a legal protest as the frantic pace of rushing against

the dawn and sleep wore on. And finally as the rays of light in the eastern sky were but a faint glow, and "Lawyer Mac" was so tired that "t-h-e" was being spelled "t-e-a" on the stencils she was cutting, the "push" ended in the office of Harvey and Wood that was dominated by the odors of a night's activities by people covered with sweat from their own hot, tired bodies. A car drove up to the office, driven by a disgustingly fresh Negro gentleman who had taken a day off from work to drive the lawyers on the 300-mile round trip from Danville to Charlottesville, where an audience would be held with Judge Michie. A telegram was sent to the *City Hall* lawyers to confirm the phone conversations made earlier—one had to give the other side notice. While Andrew Muse, Dean Robb, and Harry Wood went off to wash and change shirts for the trip to Charlottesville, Jim Lee and I went to the parsonage of the High Street Baptist Church and there got the signature of a sleepy preacher, Lendell Chase, on the suit being filed to render void the Danville picketing ordinance under which thirty-six of our people had already been arrested. These signed federal suits, complaints, were then delivered to the team of lawyers going to Charlottesville. Sometime between the full sunrise and eternity I stretched out on the office floor of Harvey and Wood near a friendly dog named Goldie and fell asleep.

In what seemed like but moments later, Jim Lee was shaking me. "Wake up! Wake up!" It was 7:45 A.M., June 18, 1963, and I had to wash, change clothes and eat in time to be in the Municipal Court of Danville by 9:00 A.M., and the Danville Corporation Court at 10:00 A.M. and perhaps jail or some other place after that. Miraculously, I came alive and stumbled dazedly over some familiar forms sprawled on top of desks or draped on chairs. This might

be the day of days, I thought to myself. I was hoping that
Judge Michie would be so mad at the flaunting of the
jurisdiction of the federal courts that he would immediately
order the release of Barksdale, stop all further proceedings
on the state court injunction, and declare the Danville
anti-picketing ordinance a disgrace . . . and that the day
would be as cool as San Francisco. This was a critical day.
It was the first opportunity for a federal-state confrontation.

Shortly after 9:00 A.M., Judge Calvin Berry found the
six sit-inners guilty . . . in Municipal Court. Appeals were
noted. At 10:00 A.M. T. Tucker, the clerk of the Corporation Court, began calling the roll of the 105 persons then
charged with violation of the injunction. There was a slight
recess then while Link and Tucker held a discussion in
Judge Aiken's chamber. We assumed they were being informed of the proceedings now set for 2:00 P.M. in Judge
Michie's chambers in Charlottesville and that Councilman
John W. Carter and City Attorney James A. H. Ferguson
had flown up there to oppose our legal moves.

The next case called for trial on the charge of violating
Aiken's injunction was that of Thurman Echols, an apt
high school senior of sixteen who had done much to make
the earlier demonstrations a success in both numbers and
discipline. Echols was a natural leader who had received
a ready response from his fellow students. This same leadership carried over into the mass meetings where Echols often
organized and led the songs and generally aided both
Reverend Dunlap and Reverend Campbell in directing the
affairs of protest. There were many adults, both in and out
of active participation in the Movement, who accepted
Echols as a leader and a "boy who is going to make us all
proud one day."

Echols had been arrested during the afternoon of June 10, 1963, and jailed. He had been asked to call his mother to come and get him. He did. She came and they jailed her on grounds of contributing to the delinquency of a minor, her son. She called her husband for help; he came and was jailed on the same charge as his wife. The pressure was on the family. His jailing had threatened his laboring job.

Jerry Williams represented Echols. The trial started after a pile of different motions had all been filed and made by Jerry attacking the constitutionality of the proceedings, the injunction, lack of a juvenile court hearing for Echols first, the police atmosphere of the court, the "search-and-seizure" tactics of the police at the courtroom door again, lack of jury trial, and lack of particulars as to what Echols was supposed to have done. Judge Aiken summarily denied each motion almost before they were made—to which action Jerry just as summarily excepted . . . almost before they were denied.

Commonwealth Attorney Eugene Link completed a direct examination of a policeman by the name of Wade who had taken some pictures of the June 10 demonstration, and Jerry was in the midst of a vigorous cross-examination when a note was passed to Judge Aiken. A recess was called with abruptness. We were startled.

"I would like to see Mr. Thurman Echols and Mr. Williams in my office," the Judge said excitedly. Jerry Williams, the Judge, a white lawyer named Theodore Huggins, and two others held a conference in the chambers of Judge Aiken. About twenty-five minutes later the conferees returned to the now tense courtroom. There was the smell of "monkey business" in the air.

At 11:45 A.M., Theodore P. Huggins, a lawyer, approached the bench with a frightened man, Thurman Echols, Sr., the father of Jerry Williams's client. Judge Aiken asked the father five critical questions as everyone sat on the edge of his seat because the questions and answers could affect Jerry Williams's future as a lawyer:

"Mr. Echols, that young man sitting over there," pointing to Jerry's client, "is that your son?"

"That's right, he's my son, yes."

"How old is he?"

"Sixteen."

"Mr. Echols, when did you make arrangements to have Mr. Theodore P. Huggins as legal counsel to represent your son in this case?"

"Just a few minutes before this case, I asked Mr. Huggins to represent my son in this—just a few minutes ago it was."

"Did you ever authorize Mr. Williams to act as legal counsel and defend your son in this case, Mr. Echols?"

"I spoke to him previously about the case, once."

"But you never authorized Mr. Jerry L. Williams to act as legal counsel to defend your son, in this case, Mr. Echols?"

"I spoke to him previously about the case, once."

"But you never authorized Mr. Jerry L. Williams to act as legal counsel to defend your son?"

There was a pause that was long enough for Jerry to have gotten angry enough to have choked a client's father. Under oath a setting had been created which would place the parent of a client in the position of saying that a lawyer had solicited a case, a racially controversial case of a young leader of the Movement, and the answer given could mean disbarment for Jerry, his professional death. And then the answer came to the Judge's question:

"No sir. I never authorized him as legal counsel to defend him. I asked but *didn't authorize him.*"

Jerry jumped into the middle of the situation and in a high pitched voice, close to a shout, began talking:

"Mr. Echols, didn't you come to me and tell me about your son? And didn't you tell me that your wife and you wanted me to defend him?" Mr. Echols nodded yes. "Isn't that what you asked me to do when your son had been in trouble? Didn't you ask me to defend him and act as legal counsel? And then Mr. Huggins came along this morning and you asked him to defend him a few minutes ago?" To all of Jerry's questions Mr. Echols nodded assent.

At first I thought Jerry was excited. I then discovered he was just mad. I moved the papers about on the counsel table after he returned and saw Jerry's "hold card": a retainer form signed by Echols' father days before this trial.

Judge Aiken ended the matter by asking, "Mr. Echols, do you want Mr. Theodore P. Huggins to defend your son in this case as you requested him to do earlier?"

"Yes, sir."

Jerry withdrew as lawyer and then Huggins spoke: "Your Honor, I would like to request a continuance in this case until tomorrow morning at which time this case will be ready for trial."

"Is that agreeable to you, Mr. Link?" Judge Aiken asked the prosecutor.

"Yes," Link, the Commonwealth Attorney, responded.

"All right, this case will be set for tomorrow," Judge Aiken said. Echols, his father, and his newly-employed attorney, Huggins, left the courtroom wading through a flood of stares from the others awaiting trial on the charge of violating the injunction. From Echols' fellow high school students—many of whom had been recruited for the demonstrations by Echols—came the deepest gaping looks into his face, the face of one who had turned back.

A link in the chain had been broken.

Time moved onward. The rest of us merely sat there on June 18, 1963, and waited for the next name to be selected whimsically for trial; we never knew which one would be next and this added to the psychological pressures, a result deliberately sought after by those who intended that there be no more protests against the orderly, calm and racially segregated patterns of Danville life which existed prior to the shouts of "Freedom!" echoing through the streets from black lips that were supposed to be happy and satisfied.

"The next case is Case No. 85, Ernest Howard Smith," T. Tucker the Clerk intoned. "Is the Commonwealth ready to proceed in the case of defendant, Ernest Howard Smith?"

"Yes," the Commonwealth Attorney Link replied.

"Is the defendant's counsel ready to defend?" the Clerk asked. I was the defense lawyer. The Clerk knew that none of the defense lawyers were ready to defend because we knew not what our clients were supposed to have done of the dozen or so offenses contained in the long state court injunction, or when their case would be called. Just as Ernest Howard Smith's name had just been called a few seconds ago he could have called my number, No. 45, which was even further up on the list the Clerk was using. The dialog between Judge Aiken and myself began:

"Your Honor, I make here the following motions that defendant's counsel is not ready to defend because: Number one, we are not ready because material notice has not been given to Mr. Smith regarding just what the charges are against him. Furthermore, adequate time is not allowed for proper preparation by legal counsel in this case. And we filed a motion for a Bill of Particulars, yesterday, which his Honor overruled. And to which we noted an exception.

"Number two, we are unready to proceed because it is the position of the attorneys for Mr. Ernest Howard Smith that the Injunction which the Court is attempting to proceed upon is unlawful. It is unlawful, because the Injunction on its face is too broad and vague; much too vague; and does not give adequate notice to defendants. Furthermore, this Injunction is unconstitutional under the First, Fifth, and Fourteenth Amendments to the Constitution; as State laws cannot be made which infringe on Constitutional rights guaranteed under these Amendments.

"Number three, we make a motion, again, that we want a trial by jury. However, your Honor has ruled that no jury trials would be allowed. Therefore, we take exception to that on the grounds that it is a Constitutional right.

"The fourth motion we would make is that these proceedings are invalid because due process of law under the statutory requirements in the State of Virginia is not being followed during these proceedings. And under the State's laws you have due process of laws normally followed in cases where you have some person who is at liberty and that nobody appeared to take out the proper warrants; then as a practical matter the Virginia Constitution and the United States Constitution have built into them certain safeguards to protect persons charged in any case.

"I refer, for example, to the Fourteenth Amendment, which is a safeguard which guarantees nobody can be put into such a position as we have been in these proceedings. There are certain safeguards such as process-serving; the proper swearing in of each and every witness. Because then if a person is properly sworn as a witness by the court and if he swears falsely to certain facts in a case, that person then becomes liable and likely for a charge of pure perjury.

"Therefore, at this point we would make a motion for a continuance on the grounds that we need a Bill of Particulars upon which to prepare our defense. Also, we find ourselves in a similar position as Mr. Huggins, the attorney who was retained earlier by Mr. Echols.

"Nevertheless, the defendants have retained us. And we ask the Court to grant to us the same privileges and consideration as Your Honor previously granted today to Mr. Huggins."

"I do not possibly see what another case has to do with this one. Motions overruled."

"Exceptions noted. Your Honor, at this time I should like to go further on record as objecting to the motion for temporary Injunction and Restraining Order, which you issued yesterday, restricting observers to attend this trial.

"We are concerned because this is supposed to be a public trial. Therefore, we make a motion to have a ruling that this "private trial" is in violation of all Constitutional rights guaranteed us under the Constitution of the United States.

"We should also like to call to the attention of this Court our continuing objections to the practices and procedures we complained of yesterday and which are in effect today. Namely, that in this Court there exists the situation where this Courtroom is dominated by policemen and a heavy display of guns.

"Even though the Court contends to rise above these things; it may perhaps be a little impressed by this show of might, unconsciously, perhaps? And we move to this Court that it take judicial notice of that fact that there are approximately twenty-five to thirty-five armed police officers here in this Courtroom this morning. A count at this time indicates there are—"

"Don't create an apprehensive atmosphere."

"There are approximately at this time eighteen police officers in this courtroom at the present time sir."

"The Court feels there is too much apprehension in the Courtroom. Overruled!"

"The defendant at this time notes exception to His Honor's ruling. The motions which we made yesterday we ask at this time—and to which we agreed yesterday would be a part of the records of all of the cases—that they in all of these cases be treated as a part of the record in each of these cases rather than repeating these same motions in each and every individual case."

"I think that is a very good idea, now, if we go ahead with the trial."

"Exception noted. We will at the proper time ask for a ruling on exclusion of witnesses, exclusion from certain rooms—"

"All right."

"And also in the Witness Room, number 418, there remain certain signs which we feel tend to operate and have an offensive influence on the jury; and to which we object."

"The jury? This is not a trial by jury."

"I assume, Your Honor, you are familiar with the racial signs?"

"That is not in my vision. This is not a jury case. And I think the signs you object to have no relation to this case. Overruled."

"Exception noted, Your Honor."

The Commonwealth Attorney presented two witnesses in proof of its case against Ernest Smith. Each of these witnesses was cross-examined at some length. In addition several pictures were introduced into evidence. At 1:00 P.M. a recess was taken until 2:30 P.M.

At 2:00 P.M., nearly one hundred and fifty miles away, Harry Wood, Dean Robb, and Andrew Muse began pushing the cause of the Danville Movement before United States District Judge Thomas Michie to secure an order from him banning further trials of those charged with violating the Corporation Court injunction, the release from the City Farm of Ezell Barksdale, and to declare the Danville anti-picketing ordinance void.

Precisely at 2:30 P.M. the trial of Smith resumed in Corporation Court and at 3:15 P.M. the Reverend Lawrence Campbell and the Reverend Lendell Chase had turned down the request of the Justice Department Attorney William A. Geoghegan and the personal telephone plea of Attorney General Robert Kennedy for a cessation of all demonstrations "so that matters can be solved." Geoghegan had arranged the meeting between the Movement Leaders and the Mayor's Advisory Committee the day before. "I'll do all in my power to stop demonstrations in order to allow the courts and the Committee to work out this situation," Geoghegan indicated.

After reading the same memorandum used the day before at the conclusion of the Barksdale trial, at 3:14 P.M., Judge Aiken sentenced Ernest Smith, forty-six years old, to pay a $50.00 fine and serve four months on the City Farm, half of the sentence being suspended on the condition that Smith have good behavior for a period of two years. It was then that Thurman Echols, Jr., appeared before Judge Aiken again. His lawyer, Huggins, indicated that Echols wanted to enter a guilty plea and that it was not necessary to have the trial set for the next day.

Echols was sworn in and then proceeded to admit that he had led the demonstration in the early part of the day on June 10 and that he was aware of the injunction. And then Huggins began a plea for leniency:

". . . The Negroes of Danville, as throughout the country, have made tremendous advancements prior to recent times through *sound leadership*. . . . But in recent times irresponsible leadership has taken over under the guise of civil liberties and nonviolence. Here is a sixteen-year-old boy looking for leadership. What leadership has led him astray? Is it the real leadership of 12,000 Negroes in Danville? Or is it a few men under indictment in this court or facing charges in other courts? Is the Negro youth of Danville being led astray by men under indictment?" asked Huggins.

". . . Misguided outside agitators have come in and swayed these people. They can tell a beautiful tale that appeals to their natural aspirations. Their motives, however, are not necessarily to help the Negro race. We have even had the spectacle of an attorney-at-law from outside the city participating in demonstrations." And on Huggins went to the appreciation of a score of city officials who had been alerted that Huggins was going to make the speech denouncing the Movement and use the guilty plea of Echols as his platform. Most of the members of the Danville City Council were present.

Looks of disgust at Huggins statements were on the faces of most of the demonstrators awaiting trial. Avon Rollins asked me, "Why do they have to grind Echols into the garbage just because he's human and weak?" City Hall went for the last ounce of castration of Echols' self-esteem. Huggins went on:

"I ask the Court to show him now that it is in the state courts that you get real justice. . . . That the state courts are where substantial justice is done." After Huggins finished, Judge Aiken turned to Echols:

"Did you hear what your lawyer said?"

"Yes," replied Echols meekly.

"Do you believe like he says you believe?"

"Yes."

"Do you expect to do what your lawyer expects you to do?"

"Yes."

"Are you sorry you got messed up in this?" "Yes," was the reply.

And then Judge Aiken had Echols' father come up before the bench. Once there, the father was asked to confirm his son's oaths of "obedience" and "penitence." Dutifully, before the awesome power of the Court, Echols' father confirmed. Echols was sentenced to fifteen days confinement, all of which was suspended; and Danville thereby served notice that anyone who would go through such a procedure would avoid being jailed without hope of bail before the sentence expired.

Shortly after that the Court adjourned for the day and all of us, defendants and lawyers, were ordered to be back in court the next day, Wednesday, June 19 at 10:00 A.M. As the hour approached 5:00 P.M. we learned that the first full-time SCLC staff member, Herbert Coulton, had arrived in town for permanent assignment. Coulton confined his activities over the next few weeks to voter registration and did a good job. When he left several weeks later there were more than six hundred new Negro voters on the Danville voter's list.

At 5:00 P.M. on June 18, 1963, the Mayor's Advisory Committee was meeting with the Retail Merchants Association, whose stores were the subject of an effective Negro boycott, and while they met twenty-nine Negro ladies demonstrated silently and minus signs in front of the downtown stores for a few minutes before being arrested. In Charlottesville, four hours' driving time away, the conference with Judge Michie ended with a date set for a full hearing of the matters raised by the Movement lawyers, the coming Monday, June 24, and Michie's expressed uncertainty about what he thought should be done. Denied was the insistence of an immediate order to free Ezell Barksdale, who had been jailed by Judge Aiken without authorization inasmuch as the removal of the Barksdale case to the federal court left Judge Aiken without lawful power to act. Though Wood, Robb, and Muse had not convinced Judge Michie that immediate relief should be granted, their arguments were powerful enough to convince Carter and Ferguson that the position of Danville would be stronger if no further trials were held. Unknown to any of us, Carter and Ferguson counseled Aiken against any further trials . . . but they were furious.

In many ways, Tuesday, June 18, 1963, was the turning point of a phase of the Movement, a critical phase. First, the five Negroes in Danville who practiced law there had shown extraordinary heroism.

Almost 100 per cent of their practice was before Judge Aiken in the Corporation Court or the two minor courts, which are strongly influenced by *City Hall. City Hall* opposed the Movement and endorsed all steps taken to crush the Movement and the people in it. Their professional lives as lawyers in Danville placed them before Judge Aiken— the sole judge presiding in the court of record, Danville's Corporation Court. Judge Aiken was a strong moving party in all that these five Negro lawyers were now opposing, in a town so small that the Corporation Court handled nothing but civil cases one month (civil cases are property and domestic disputes regarding such things as ownership of land, recovery of money debts, and divorces) and the next month it handled nothing but criminal cases.

Over both the civil and criminal terms Judge Aiken presided.

There aren't, unhappily, many lawyers in America who would have bucked *City Hall* under such awesome dangers, but these five lawyers did it.

All five of the lawyers were closely associated with the NAACP and its legal staff (as one told me: NAACP born, NAACP bred and NAACP until dead). They had in effect been told not to have anything to do with removal petitions for their clients and to conduct an entirely separate defense from that of one of the NAACP's most ardent critics, the person they called affectionately: "Snake Doctor." Both admonitions were disregarded.

And why?

First, I think they saw that the only way they could hope to keep their clients out of jail after the summary way in which my client, Barksdale, was sentenced, confined, and denied bail, was to remove the cases to the Federal Court. So they did it. Secondly, they saw that the only way they could hope to minimize monstrous display of naked power by *City Hall* was to combine what legal resources were available—postponing the internecine hassle until the "cool of the evening."

From the evening of June 17, 1963, on, everything was done cooperatively among the lawyers. Everyone freely assigned tasks to the teams of lawyers from northern cities rotating over two-week periods. Everyone did everything. However, on a few occasions, when there was a particularly odious task to be performed, "odious" in the sense that although the task was ethically and legally essential, it had unusually traumatic potential with *City Hall,* I would usually insist on doing it because I knew that one day—soon—I would leave Danville behind for another hot spot. . . .

Or perhaps a cold one.

People wondered why all 105 of the defendants called before Corporation Court for alleged violation of the injunction didn't have lawyers. The answer was provided by the experience earlier on this day with Thurmond Echols. Echols was no stronger or weaker than anyone else connected with the Danville Movement, whether that person was layman, lawyer, or pistol-whipped SNCC staff member who was a veteran of Mississippi. But Echols was subjected to cruel and unusual pressures. *City Hall* had power. If Jerry Williams had approached Echols to represent him, a procedure permissible when one is charged with a crime and can't get a lawyer, in all but controversial cases such as this one, Jerry would have faced disbarment, a "professional death." All during the active weeks of the Danville protest the ears of the lawyers were sullied with this threat.

And the second way in which Tuesday, June 18, 1963, was the beginning of a new phase of the Danville Movement was that the lawyers had captured the spirit of protest and had in the framework of their legal training (all or almost all of us were graduates of the civil rights-orientated Howard University Law School, and had been taught by Professor James Nabrit) implemented the philosophy of the greatest Abolitionist, Frederick Douglass:

"He is whipped mostest, who's whipped easiest."

We had fought back and taken the offensive. We had filed a suit in the federal court attacking the validity of the Danville anti-picketing ordinance and also removed the balance of the cases of those charged with violating the injunction to the federal courts. As my partner Joe Jordon often says, "We must teach City Hall that he who fights, shall be fought." We were fighting. This action had enhanced the probability of intervention of the federal government. Furthermore, we hoped by this action to avoid the slow, devious, and deceitful path of appealing the hundreds of cases through the courts of a southern state where often justice for a Negro is either a miracle, an accident, or both. This became pattern for the future. As Danville would pass or invoke a law, the lawyers would scamper to the federal courts with a suit. Unemployment compensation was denied to several persons indiscriminately arrested by the police: a federal suit was filed. Danville passed and used an anti-parade ordinance: a federal suit was filed. It invoked the "John Brown" statute: a federal suit was filed.

By our conduct on June 18 we recognized that in the federal courts we had a chance, and not the ghost of one in state courts.

Another milestone was passed that day when there was a demonstration by twenty-nine ladies in spite of the efforts of William A. Geoghegan of the Justice Department and the personal phone call to the Movement leaders by Attorney General Robert Kennedy. The presence of the Justice Department representative in addition to a beefed-up contingent of FBI agents was indication that the news about Danville was reaching a wide audience to the North of Virginia and that pressure was mounting on the federal government to aid Danville's brutalized Negroes.

There being the usual counter-pressure not to act in Virginia from high sources (including Sen. Harry F. Byrd and other members of the Virginia Congressional delegation in key positions), the Kennedy administration responded in characteristic fashion. It responded in the same fashion as it had responded in Savannah, Ga.; Greenwood, Miss.; Birmingham, Ala.; Cambridge, Md.; and other communities engaged in racial protest. First it brought about a cessation of demonstration, if possible, and then it wielded pressure on city hall or local merchants to make minor concessions. The third step consisted of convincing the persons involved in racial protest that they had gained a *great* victory while simultaneously persuading city hall or the merchants that they had given up nothing important. To understand how difficult it is for a Negro leader to say "No" to the federal government one must be able to conceive of an almighty God who is omnipresent and omnipotent. Subtract 10 per cent of that image of God and you have the Negro's image of the United States government.

Lastly, June 18 was a momentous day because of Thurmond Echols. Coincidentally or otherwise, Thurmond Echols was brought before Judge Aiken in the Danville Corporation Court at a time that all of the persons then charged with violating the injunction were present, and at a time after Ezell Barksdale had been led off to jail and denied bail pending appeal of his sentence. The defense lawyers and those they were defending knew about the pressures on Echols.

They knew that it was very important for Echols to be out of jail because he desired so to attend the segregated summer school for Negro students at Langston High. They knew that his mother had been arrested when she came to bail him out. They knew that his father had been arrested when he came to jail to get both his wife and son and that this jailing had created serious problems for the father who thought that he might lose a sorely needed job. Those awaiting trial were as frightened as Echols and didn't relish serving a month or more at the rock pile of the City Farm. In every way Echols was understood and sympathized with in his predicament which was similar to many others.

From what happened, it was obvious that *City Hall* didn't know this.

As those sitting in the courtroom watched the ceremony of bringing Echols up before everyone, including a hastily assembled gathering of city employees and city officials; as they saw the white lawyer assert what Echols' plea would be, guilty; as they saw Echols terrifyingly make that plea of guilty; as they heard Lawyer Huggins' extended peroration which excoriated, ridiculed, belittled, and maligned the Movement, its leadership, and methods, those in the many seats assigned to the defendants could hear the cries of anguish on the night of June 10, 1963, as muscular police-men unceasingly flailed with hard clubs on black skulls and bodies as if they were killing—or trying to kill—snakes . . . the spectacle of pleading guilty before that judge, in that court, and begging for mercy became as repulsive to them as it would have been to watch the bodies of their mothers consumed by a lynch mob.

From the point of view of *City Hall* the matter was a mistake. It would have been far better if Echols had been taken into chambers, and if quietly and privately the Court had accepted his plea and turned him loose.

So nauseating was that scene—which was never re-peated—that out of more than seven hundred persons ar-rested for demonstrating in Danville that summer, fewer than a baker's dozen ever pleaded guilty.

At the conclusion of the day in the Corporation Court, June 18, and a hasty meal at Oliver's Cafe on Spring Street, full efforts of the lawyers in town were devoted to prepara-tion for either the coming federal court hearing in Danville on Monday, June 24, 1963, or the appeal to the Virginia

Court of Appeals to get bail for Ezell Barksdale and Ernest Howard Smith pending the hearing of their full appeal. Sam W. Tucker, who had a Richmond office, where the Virginia Court of Appeals is located, agreed to present the application for bail. In tandems, our names for the first time appeared on the same legal document. The united legal approach forged of necessity in Danville had spread to the state level.

After some more interviews with witnesses and clients scheduled for trial the next morning in the Danville Municipal Court, Jim Lee and seven very tired lawyers hied themselves off to bed shortly after midnight.

CHAPTER 13

Bitter Laughs

Ace,
I'm not lying
Smile's phony
Laughing for no crying.

No screams, stifle lacrimal flow
Though dying
Mock!
Laugh like hell!

No crying.
—Asininity 1/10, "The Wisdom of Dawley"

The following afternoon, Wednesday, June 19, while eating at Oliver's, we read mixed news in the Danville *Bee*. One story told about Alabama State Troopers using cattle prods to rout three hundred Negroes from the lawn of the Etowah County Courthouse in Gadsden. Instinct told us that many of our friends (who also happened to be clients in the *Gadsden Omnibus Integration Suit*) were among those three hundred. The second item was pleasant. It announced that the Virginia Pupil Placement Board had assigned ten Negro students to Danville's previously all-white schools. Lee and I laughed. All ten of the students were children of those leading the Movement.

Earlier that same day we had appeared in Municipal

Court, where our clients, as usual, were convicted and had, as usual, noted appeals to the Corporation Court. Shortly after the roll call, the lawyers and those charged with violating the Corporation Court injunction were "excused" and told to report back at 10:00 A.M. the next day, Thursday, June 20. Among the lawyers this unsought continuance caused a chuckle. We knew that the Corporation Court wasn't going to try any cases until Judge Michie had ruled, but didn't want to give the impression that the Corporation Court recognized it didn't have the right to call the defendants before it. It was easier for us to appear and answer roll call under the unlawful exercise of power than to contest bail forfeitures.

Those chuckles changed to surprise when we saw members of the special Grand Jury hastily convening. The afternoon paper suggested there would be more indictments because "new demonstration leaders have emerged." None of us got excited about the matter, especially me. I didn't consider myself a leader and had my hands full just trying to keep abreast of the scores of legal problems that each day presented.

Back at the office of Harvey and Wood, which was the legal headquarters for the Movement *de facto* though not yet *de jure*, a call had been received that Sam Tucker had appeared before a justice of the Virginia Supreme Court of Appeals on the matter of bail for Barksdale and Smith, who had been held without bail, and the justice had refused to act with the dispatch we thought the statute required of him. The matter of bail for Barksdale and Smith had been "taken under advisement" without indication of how long that would be.

The news was discussed by all of us (Dean Robb, Ruth Harvey, Nat Conyers, George Woody, Jim Lee, Harry Wood,

A. C. Muse, Jerry Williams, and myself) and accepted glumly. We began to question ourselves as lawyers. With our *all* we couldn't get two men out on bail who had been jailed by a court with no more *lawful* power over them than "Cock Robin."

After a short conference it was decided to forgo an immediate appeal to the United States Supreme Court for bail in favor of pushing the matter before Judge Michie again, at the hearing set in Danville for the coming Monday, June 24, 1963. Though phone calls had been made to Bill Kunstler and Art Kinoy in New York, Professor Charles Antieu in Washington, George Crockett in Detroit, and Sam Tucker in Richmond, notifying them of the coming hearing in federal court on Monday, and even though they made most of the preparation, we had to do lots of evidence-gathering, marshaling of witnesses, summarizing court appearances, securing the services of court reporters and answering questions flooding the office via telephone and in person. The day ended the following morning, June 20, at 1:00 A.M., when Nat Conyers made this observation:

"This work, and a whole lot more, will be here tomorrow. It won't go away. Let's go home," and yawned deeply. Harry Wood rose to the challenge.

"Nat, you're brilliant!" This provoked laughter which far exceeded the merits of the little ribbing Harry had subjected Nat to for saying what all thought. But when one is tired and his body feels as if it were an alligator's with a long tail dragging, normal restraints aren't operative. Things were secured and we left . . . dropping tired bodies into beds like globs of soft clay and dying until roused hours later for another round with *City Hall*.

Like many days before, June 20, 1963, began with our appearance before Judge Calvin Berry in Municipal Court.

Some twenty-nine persons arrested for demonstrating the day before appeared briefly, indicated who their attorneys were, and had their cases continued because the anti-picketing ordinance under which they were being charged was under challenge before the federal court. At 10:00 A.M. in Corporation Court, four flights above the Municipal Court, the roll was called of persons charged with violating the injunction, now 135, and a severe blow was dealt to the local Negro lawyers by Judge Aiken. We were informed that every lawyer and every defendant had to be in Corporation Court every day court was in session. The hope had been that on days when a client of one of the local lawyers was not on trial, that the local lawyer could devote his attention to private practice. This was important because one day, when the demonstration cases would end, one needed a practice to return to. Furthermore, Dr. King's SCLC, the Gandhi Society and all other parties had yet to perform meaningfully financially.

The spokesmen for *City Hall's* point of view, the local papers, recognized the effect of the ruling: "A 'day in court' that could be extended into weeks has been assured the multitude of defendants still awaiting trial on contempt charges arising from Judge A. M. Aiken's injunction . . ." It also fell hard on many of the defendants who were employed—or hoped to be—and were supporting families.

The news of the previous day had created a small crisis for the power complex of Danville. Ten students, all children of persons connected with the Movement, had been ordered admitted to white schools. Danville didn't want the impression to be created that the demonstrations had caused these assignments. Mayor Stinson explained, "As for the State Pupil Placement Board's action in transferring certain Negro children to white schools in Danville, I want it distinctly understood that it was the Board's action based on applications filed some time ago and has no connection whatsoever with the recent violation of the law in Danville."

This was amusing. It was well known that the Pupil Placement Board didn't assign Negroes to white schools unless it was under a court order or the local school board recommended the assignment.

After leaving the Corporation Court there were cases down the hall in Juvenile Court that had to be continued again; everything could be affected by the pending decision of Judge Michie on the removal and such other actions that were being prepared by us to present in federal Court, Monday, June 24, 1963.

After a quick lunch and a short conference in the High Street Baptist church with the 135 persons then charged with violating the injunction, all legal hands headed for the office of Harvey and Wood to continue the preparation for the coming Monday.

As the long distance calls flowed in from George Crockett and Ernie Goodman in Detroit, Sam Tucker in Richmond, and Kunstler and Kinoy in New York, all told us that there was a lot of "corn to be plowed" to satisfy the needs of Monday when Judge Michie would come to Danville. Harry Wood began working on a federal suit to be filed to stop the local unemployment commission from denying checks to those persons with charges against them. Nat Conyers and Dean Robb were concentrating on gathering evidence of the atrocities committed by the Danville police—including the night of June 10, 1963. Muse and Ruth Harvey were giving their attention to a federal suit seeking a declaration by Judge Michie that the Corporation Court injunction issued by Judge Aiken was no good. My attention was directed toward preparing an attack in federal court on the validity of the "John Brown" law. Others in the office were being snatched by requests of one kind or another by those working on specific assignments. It was close to 4:00 P.M. and as I started biting my fingernails and scratching my head to stir a tired brain, I was informed that one of the incessant flow of phone calls was for me: "Pick it up, Len. It's an emergency," "Lawyer Mac" (Miss A. D. McCain), the office secretary, brusquely demanded. Two SNCC staffers had been subpoenaed to appear before the special Grand Jury of the Corporation Court: Daniel Foss and Robert Zellner.

In the Renault I scooted down to City Hall and went straight to the fourth floor to the Corporation Court where the Grand Jury was having its hearing in the room that had the four racially designated toilets.

My instructions to the two men were short and simple: Allow yourself to be sworn in, give your name, take the initiative by asking the Grand Jury to give you some idea about what questions they want to ask you, listen without making any further statements, and then refuse to answer any questions, stating merely, "I invoke my privilege against self-incrimination." To make sure that they had it I had them repeat it softly, "I invoke my privilege against self-incrimination."

Special emphasis was given to not saying anything about the Fifth Amendment. They were told that the "Fifth" applied to the federal government and they were now appearing before an agency of the state government. "Now repeat again," I told them. They responded, after giving a look that indicated they were irked with the parrot-like repetition I was asking for, "I invoke my privilege against self-incrimination." Then for two or three minutes I cautioned them about the worst thing they could do in such a setting: answer questions.

Examples were given about persons who were convicted of perjury for testimony given before a grand jury even though they had told no lies. I found most effective a case I knew about in which a party was asked if he knew a fellow whom I shall call Willie Pluto. Thinking that he had nothing to hide, he told the truth and said "no." He was indicted and convicted by a jury in Montgomery, Ala., which refused to believe that the landlord of his rooming house was known to him as *Wilbur Whitsett,* though he was in fact named *Willie Pluto.* It was emphasized that *they should not answer questions.*

"In a courtroom the truth is only of value if it's believed. A lie that is believed has the same evaluation in a jury's mind as the truth," I told them. "Shut up! Make sure that you don't answer any questions."

Shortly after the brief instruction session was finished a bailiff came and ordered them, one by one, into the room with the racial toilet signs. As Bob Zellner and then Daniel Foss came out I asked them what questions they had been asked, made notes, and then returned to the office on South Main Street where the other lawyers were busily working.

I handed my notes to Jim Lee who looked at them while I stepped into the back of the suite of offices for a cup of coffee from an ever-ready pot that Harry Wood maintained for the constant emergencies that existed in Danville. On my return to the front office, where I began taking off my bow tie and loosening my shirt collar so as not to be overcome by the roasting heat—a heat that persisted even though the sun was far in the West—Jim spoke.

"Snake Doctor, I'm not a professional investigator or detective, as you know," he said with a small smile on his face. "I just volunteer a little time now and then when I can be spared from the blood bank. But it looks to me from

these notes on the questions asked Foss and Zellner that a
lot of people are going to be indicted."

"Tell me something new, Jim," I answered lackadaisically.

"Well, it appears that three of them are Foss, Zellner,
and Holt."

I stared in disbelief.

The small Coronella cigar fell from my mouth.

"You're nuts!" I accused Jim, somewhat frightened and
excited because it had dawned on me that he was right. I
was stunned but began a sick laugh to myself. It was sick
because I was remembering the many times I had walked
into jails, lock-ups and even prisons to interview clients to
have them tell me, "I haven't done a thing, not a thing." On
hearing this I had never laughed at them or informed them
that I didn't believe it. My approach was simply to pretend
I hadn't heard and to continue the interview with a mind un-
cluttered by the "myth" they had just uttered. Now I could
only come out with a sick laugh, a joke on myself.

Jim conveyed his impressions to the others. They didn't
accept his inference from my notes.

I did.

Jim Lee and I had known each other since 1945 when
we met in the Navy Hospital Corpsmen School in San Diego
where our black skins and indignation at the racial segregation made us seek refuge in each other's friendship. Lee was
always highly analytical. In somewhat the same way that
Indians were supposed to do when they saw a bent leaf, or
an animal's footprint and tell a great deal, Lee could take a
casual statement by the Captain's orderly, a strange truck,
or the laying-in of a large supply of liquor by an officer, and
predict with accuracy cancelling of weekend liberty, emergency transfer of corpsmen before the end of their scheduled
training period to some short-handed hospital ship, or the

coming of an Admiral aboard. While the others argued with Jim's conclusions, I busied myself calling those who would probably be indicted along with me. If Jim's hunch was right the list was long; every name meant at least $5,000 in bond money.

Bond money in Danville came mostly from dedicated local persons who would pledge their homes as security. There had been a lot of people arrested, a lot of bonds posted. It would take considerable effort to raise all the money needed.

I wasn't prepared for an indictment and to prevent my tenseness and irritability from inconveniencing others I withdrew and kept to myself for the rest of the night. Sensing this, the others let me be. "Ain't that a bitch, I'm going to be indicted," I told myself. Finally I went home and went to bed much earlier than usual. It was only 11:30 P.M.

At 9:00 A.M. the next morning, Friday, June 21, I was once again before Judge Calvin Berry in the Municipal Court. My clients were Bob Zellner, the Reverend Lendell W. Chase, Charles Echols, Bruce Baines, and Miss Annie Mae Farmer. A minor "victory" occurred when efforts to secure dismissal of all charges resulted in getting one dropped: an assault count against Zellner who had flashed his camera in the face of Chief McCain while taking McCain's picture just before the beatings began on the night of June 10, 1963. The procedures before Judge Berry in Municipal Court had become so routine that as he passed sentence he would say after each: "And Mr. Holt notes an appeal."

The Danville SCLC, the Movement, issued a news release, at about the same time that the trials were concluding in Municipal Court on June 21, indicating that the world-famous opera and concert star, Camilla Williams, was returning to Danville to give a benefit performance for the Movement and that local organizations participating in the Movement in addition to the Danville SCLC were the local NAACP and the Ministerial Alliance. National organizations cooperating with the Movement were listed as SNCC, SCLC, and CORE.

That afternoon, sensing my tenseness because I believed Jim Lee's prediction—the disbelieving Nat Conyers, Dean Robb, and Harry Wood joined Lee in ordering me to take my notes on the "John Brown" law and "Get out of the office. Get out of town. And go somewhere and get drunk. We're tired of looking at such a sick specimen."

My resistance was token, at best. I caught a plane and went to New York. A call came about 9:45 P.M., June 21, 1963. It revealed that Jim Lee was either a prophet . . . or the son of one. Minus the signature of Martin C. Martin, the lone Negro member, the special Grand Jury of the Corporation Court had added eleven more names to those of Julius Adams, Lawrence G. Campbell and Alexander I. Dunlap as indictees under the "John Brown" statute which carried a minimum punishment of five years and a maximum of ten years:

> James Forman—SNCC
> Avon Rollins—SNCC
> Robert Zellner—SNCC
> Dorothy Miller—SNCC
> Daniel Foss—SNCC
> Lendell W. Chase—SCLC
> Milton A. Reid—SCLC
> Curtis W. Harris—SCLC
> Hildreth McGhee—SCLC
> William Gray
> Len Holt

Danville's power complex had noted how the earlier indictment of Julius Adams and the Reverends Dunlap and Campbell had caused these persons to restrict, somewhat, their open involvement in demonstrations. *City Hall* had also noted that the bringing of arrests under Aiken's injunction had little effect because the people in the Movement believed it to be just as legally invalid as Councilman Carter knew it to be. These further indictments were brought to chop off any, and all, persons believed to be exerting leadership in any phase of the protest. The logic was that an intimidated leadership would be either no leadership or controllable leadership. Hence, the number indicted under the John Brown law was increased from the original three to fourteen. The fact that nary a soul had done the slightest act or thought to justify an indictment was irrelevant. When one has power, use it. *City Hall* did.

The next day, Saturday, June 22, a weird tale was broadcast nation-wide. It involved Danville's slogan of being the "City of One Hundred Churches" (37 Negro, 63 white); it summarized the invasion by the Danville police of the sanctuary of the High Street Baptist Church. At 8:45 A.M. the police went upstairs to the church office, kicked the office door open, and arrested Avon Rollins, Bob Zellner, and Daniel Foss. To satisfy the Danville concept of piety in God's house the police offered two explanations that were widely accepted—even by some Negroes: "Through a window built into the wall of the room, police could observe several persons, amongst whom were Zellner, Foss, and Rollins, the latter holding a revolver pointing toward the (office) door." Seconds later the door was kicked open—a very heroic act under the circumstances. Mayor Stinson admitted that no gun was found nor was any looked for. The second explanation was that those arrested "were quite obviously not using the church as a place of worship."

It is not known whether or not credit for this unusual statement about the arrest should be given to Robert Gardiner, the public relations man Danville borrowed from Dan River Mills. Regardless of who should be given credit, the message was sufficient to provide the white community of Danville with assurances that its passiveness was proper.

On Monday, June 24, I returned to Danville for the hearings in federal court that continued in part on to Tuesday. Wednesday, June 26, the newspapers carried the story that the Democrats had selected Atlantic City for the site of its 1964 convention and I was arrested that night, for the second time in Danville, under the recent indictment handed down by the special Grand Jury of the Corporation Court. The first arrest had occurred 12 days earlier, June 14, on the charge of violating the Corporation Court injunction. In jail I joined a royal host which included Ivanhoe Donaldson of SNCC and the venerable jail bird, Daniel Foss. There I remained until the evening of June 28 when Michael Standard flew in from New York City to bail me.

The thought of bail having to come from so far and from so remote a source disturbed us. Why, when *Jet* Magazine and other news media were carrying articles about tens of thousands of dollars being raised by Dr. Martin Luther King in speaking engagements in places like Los Angeles, Detroit, and Westport, did his Atlanta office consistently assert that there was no money for bail for the Danville affiliate because the Atlanta office was "broke"?

Anyway one looked at it, the battle lines were drawn, and sink or swim, the Danville Movement, led by the Danville affiliate of the SCLC, had to make it on its own.

"God bless the child who's got his own . . ."

CHAPTER 14

"D" Day

> *Watch that gal*
> *Shake that thing*
> *Everybody can't be*
> *a Martin Luther King.*
> —Julian Bond

Since the beginning of the Danville Movement the one figure who was the unseen guest at every mass meeting, the standard by which all deeds were measured, the Big Brother, the ultimate weapon that would insure that *City Hall* would not prevail, was Martin Luther King.

In March of 1963, when King had appeared, Negroes had flooded-out the biggest auditorium in the City of Danville, the Armory. It had been a turn-away crowd situation with every available seat filled.

Every word in the paper, every fleeting glimpse of King on television, was consumed with passion in Danville and widely discussed: "Dr. King really told them white folks off." "They know better'n to mess with Dr. King," and similar approbations were common.

When the big *Putsch* came in Birmingham, black Danville, became—almost as a group—dial switchers during the evening television news trying to catch the words and pictures about Birmingham on each of the four stations feeding into Danville. So closely did they follow the Birmingham events that there were persons who, on any given day, could quote the number of arrests, the number bitten by dogs, and the other statistics. In an aura of victory the Birmingham demonstrations ended in the middle of May, 1963 . . . and served as a catalyst for demonstrations all over the South. In the Danville Negro community, as in so many other places, the Birmingham protest added to our concept of King as both a legend and myth that walked on earth. A seventy-eight-year-old demonstrator in Danville named Daniel McCain, with whom I shared a cell on my second Danville jailing described Dr. Martin Luther King in these terms: "He's a man who's well named."

At every mass meeting in the Danville season of protest there were references to Dr. Martin Luther King: "On the phone today, Dr. King told me to tell you, 'Walk together Children, don't get weary,'" or "As soon as the final touches are put on the Birmingham agreement, Dr. King is headed this way." In the middle of May the Birmingham protests ended. On the last of May the Danville protests began. From the beginning, everyone involved knew that Dr. King was coming to lead the Danville protest; the only uncertainty was the date.

On June 28, 1963, this fever of anticipation soared because for the first time since March, Dr. King was back in Virginia, in a town called Suffolk. It didn't matter that Suffolk was 170 miles away; it was still Virginia. Before a throng of 5,000 persons, in a speech broadcast by radio to a large part of southern Virginia and a vast section of northern North Carolina, King called for a mass descent on Danville on July 3 and promised to arrive in Danville himself that day with his entire task force. Negro citizens in Danville, for the most part, received the news with unbounded joy. Reflecting the exuberance of those around us, Harry Wood and I toasted "The coming of the King" with large steins of beer in the protective confines of Oliver's Cafe.

If King could help—and he could—his help was sorely needed. The list of persons arrested in demonstrations and charged with violating the Corporation Court injunction had swollen to over 200. Bond money was drying up like the mouths of prisoners left in the City Farm "hot box." Massive demonstration in Danville had been reduced to a trickle. With nearly $300,000 in local property pledged as bail, the unlikelihood of more mass demonstrations was apparent. The efforts of the Justice Department, through its representative Harold J. Flannery, to get several restaurants to desegregate or one or two jobs for Negroes with the City had been rebuffed and the Justice Department man was threatened: "In Danville, I can have you arrested . . ."

June 28 and Dr. Martin Luther King's speech in Suffolk marked the end of the close of the first phase of Danville's summer of protest and the beginning of the second phase. During the first month of action the following general developments had occurred:

First, one could detect that the fluidity and shock of the original situation had disappeared, both for the Movement and for *City Hall;* the day-to-day crisis had been routinized.

Mornings, before the Municipal, Juvenile, and Corporation courts, some demonstrators would be hauled in unceremoniously, tried, found guilty and note appeals with the benefit of local Negro counsel and one or two out-of-town lawyers serving a two-week tour.

Later during the day some more demonstrators would picket, sit-in, or parade, and be arrested efficiently by bored cops and confined in jail until a bond of $1,500 or more was raised for each demonstrator. Afternoons somebody would meet with somebody else: The Movement would meet with *City Hall,* the Movement would meet with the merchants, or the Movement would meet with itself to resolve increasing tensions and internecine strife that occur, inevitably, when one group (called the leaders) in their wisdom makes plans to be carried out by other persons (called the organizers) without consulting—and vice-versa.

Evenings there would be a mass meeting, often with a guest speaker from out of town, who would exhort and encourage; visiting lawyers would be introduced; announcements would be made; a collection would be taken.

New city ordinances would be passed to meet a new tactic of the Movement, or an ancient statute in the criminal code would be revived and invoked—and the lawyers would try to stop the use of the law in a suit filed in federal court. *City Hall* would promote some new lie in the paper about the Movement.

And always Dr. Martin Luther King would be coming.

On June 28, 1963, he announced, "I shall be an involved participant."

At the beginning of the demonstrations, on May 31, the Movement had announced its political objectives as being the creation of a biracial committee, employment of Negroes throughout all city jobs (firemen, policemen, clerks, etc.) and in previously denied capacities with private employers (clerks, salesmen, guards, etc.), and the removal of all racial restrictions in public accommodations. The Movement had clearly failed to achieve these announced political objectives and clearly could not do so without massive outside intervention from either the federal government or Dr. Martin Luther King, or both, to offset the forces available to *City Hall.*

By June 28, those willing to demonstrate had dwindled down to a hard core of students under the tutelage of the SNCC staff members, veterans of Tennessee, Georgia, and Mississippi. Attendance at the nightly mass meetings was down, there being little new either said or done. However, the number of sympathizers for the Movement was still quite large; some indication of its size was given by a full-page advertisement in support of the Movement which ran in the Danville *Bee* and contained 1,000 names.

In short, on June 28, 1963, the Movement had survived, and done little more than survive.

This survival is attributable in no small part to the acumen of the Reverend Lendell W. Chase, president of the Danville SCLC, and the Reverend Doyle Thomas. By nature these men are conservative "middle-class" Negroes. And if this protest movement was anything, it wasn't conservative or middle class. In other words, the Movement was uncouth in the full meaning of that word. At first *City Hall* had hoped that these two men would act as a wedge to prevent a semblance of Negro unity in condemning the intransigence of *City Hall* in satisfying the Negro demands. Chase and Thomas demonstrated. City Hall accepted this only as a necessary step in the two men assuming leadership of emotional and soul-wrenching protests against segregation. When Chase and Thomas revealed that their only objections to the demonstrations led by Campbell, Adams, and Dunlap were such minor things as the absence of ties and white shirts on the males and the volume of the cries of "Freedom" before the sacred Confederate statue of Mayor Wooding . . . there was consternation.

City Hall had relied on the assumption that Chase and Thomas were more *pacific* than Dunlap, Campbell and Adams. When Chase and Thomas, in the role of leaders,

banded together with Campbell and the others and refused
to stop all demonstrations as a condition of negotiation, they
were arrested, mugged, fingerprinted and classified by *City
Hall* as "criminals unfit to talk with."

On June 28, 1963, the city government and the police,
for their part, were perfecting the machinery of oppression.
A bragging Danville policeman told Matthew Jones, SNCC
staff member assigned to Danville, "Chief's been talking to
Chief Pritchett and you know what that means." Pritchett is
the head of the Albany, Ga., police force. Mass brutality was
abandoned by Danville, thereby minimizing the possibility
of FBI investigation and the presence of outside reporters.
Less dramatic and more corrosive tactics were adopted:
constant surveillance of the Movement headquarters located
in a storefront at 226 Union Street, constant trailing of Movement people by police cruisers, a flurry of traffic arrests, midnight raids on the homes of persons known to be housing
"outside agitators," massive police scrutiny of the nightly
public meetings, withholding of unemployment insurance
due those charged with demonstrating by state officials in
charge of administering federal funds, expulsion from the
public housing project, firings by private employers, revoca-
tion of cab licenses, enforcing economic loss on those
charged with demonstrating by forcing their repeated appearance in courts while knowing that no trials were possible, raising the amount of bonds required for those arrested
to the point that persons such as Chase, Adams, Rollins, Matt
Jones, Zellner, and others were soon almost "worth their
weight in gold."

At this time it seemed there was not one local white
person with the slightest criticism of the patently septic situation. In this context the announcement that Martin Luther

King was going to be in Danville caused atrophied hopes to resurge.

But not everyone's joy was unbounded at the news of the coming of King and his task force. Vice-Mayor George B. Anderson was quoted in the paper as saying: "Local police, supplemented by a large contingent of state troopers, will be quite able to cope with any problems resulting from local or statewide efforts to force Danville to capitulate to the unreasonable demands of a small portion of the City's Negro population."

Reflecting a growing resentment in being excluded from the Movement's decision-making process and the attendant loss of power and prestige of the local NAACP, the Reverend Doyle Thomas cast aside the front of unity and condemned the leadership of King from the pulpit. Thomas asserted that the local people could handle the situation and accused King of selfishly seeking projection and glory. Few were moved by either the veiled threats of the *City Hall* or the critique of Thomas; King was coming. King was coming with his task force in response to more than four weeks of pleading for his personal intervention into Danville by the Movement leaders.

On July 1, 1963, when *City Hall* denied the Reverend Chase a parade permit to have a parade from High Street Baptist Church to Peters Park, where the rally was scheduled to be held, and when even the park itself was condemned by the folks downtown and therefore could not be used as the site of the proposed July 3 statewide mass meeting—little, if any, of the hope and enthusiasm dissipated.

July 2, 1963, was characterized in Movement language as "Pat-on-the-head, kick-in-the-pants" day. The "Pat" came after a stormy session in Municipal Court before Judge Cal-

vin Berry during which I was knocked down by Assistant
Commonwealth Attorney, Larry Wilson, as he snatched from
my hand a note attached to a warrant on Campbell which
stated that Judge Aiken didn't want Campbell admitted to
bail. Jerry Williams informed me that the U.S. Justice Department had filed, that morning, a "friend of the court" or
Amicus brief with Judge Michie, asking that the cases removed be kept in federal court and not returned to Judge
Aiken because Danville Negroes could not get a fair trial in
Aiken's court. To this "Pat" the reaction was predictable and
swift.

To a man the Danville lily white bar association de-
nounced Kennedy and supported Aiken—although *privately*
several of the white lawyers were pleased. And then the
editorials lashed out:

> BOBBY KENNEDY, instead of seeking and ascertaining the
> fact and law in the local situation, has stooped to parroting the
> careless mouthings of Len Holt. . . .

Whatever joy that was generated by the action of the
Justice Department on July 2 was short-lived. At 5:00 P.M.
on July 2, 1963, Judge Michie acted. He acted in the same
manner as one of his colleagues on the federal bench, Judge
Robert Elliot, had acted in Albany, Ga., the year before, by
rendering a federal injunction against a Negro protest movement on the grounds that the protest denied others in the
community federally protected rights. Martin Luther King
was enjoined; SNCC was enjoined; SCLC was enjoined;
CORE was enjoined; the Movement was enjoined; certain
named individuals were enjoined; and once again I was
named along with those giving leadership—and enjoined, a
form of flattery. All involved in the Movement who once

thought so well of the federal courts began a re-evaluation. Mary King, SNCC staffer handling public relations for the Danville Movement, typed a lyric and hung it on the wall of the cubicle where she worked:

> Some men ride through the night and wear white robes
> Others sit on high benches and wear black ones.

As soon as it was learned that the federal court had enjoined the Movement, the information was conveyed to Martin Luther King, in Atlanta, who was to fly up the next day for the statewide rally with his task force. Based on King's reaction when a similar federal court injunction had been entered against him and the Albany, Ga., Movement, his response was predictable.

He cancelled.

Organizational problems within SCLC were reported as the reason for his remaining in Atlanta. The Movement leaders valiantly tried to bolster waning spirits by informing the people that this was only a postponement of King's coming.

The rally the next day was held in the athletic field of the colored high school, whose facilities were graciously granted to the Movement by *City Hall* when the King threat disappeared. It was obvious to a lot of people that *City Hall* was no longer blundering about, but planning. Or perhaps the credit should go to that call supposedly placed to Chief Pritchett in Albany, Ga.

At the rally on July 3, 1963, which was poorly attended, the Reverend Fred Shuttlesworth, president of the Southern Conference Educational Fund (SCEF) and official of SCLC, showed no perturbance at the presence of three squad cars of policemen, including Chief McCain, which parked by the speaker's platform. In scathing terms he spoke his opinions of Danville, the federal and state injunctions, the federal and state judges. "I thought that federal courts supported people's freedom. I assumed that this court is too, but if he isn't, there are some boys higher than this federal judge," Shuttlesworth declared.

Shuttlesworth read excerpts from Judge Michie's restraining order and added sarcastic comments. One section of the injunction prohibited upsetting noises. "If singing 'We Shall Overcome,' is upsetting, let's upset the *hell* out of Danville! It needs to be upset when it keeps people down."

The people of Danville were told by Shuttlesworth that Martin Luther King and the task force of "lawyers, clergymen, civil rights fighters will be in Danville next week." Hopes were rekindled . . . somewhat. Large numbers of state troopers hung around the City Hall building looking bored.

Calls regarding the hastily granted federal injunction had been made to both George Crockett and Ernest Goodman in Detroit, of the Guild's CLAS, and to Bill Kunstler and Arthur Kinoy of New York. Immediate action was begun on the matter. Kunstler had caused a similar federal injunction against the Albany Movement and Martin Luther King to be flushed away the year before. A hearing on the Danville federal injunction was set for Tuesday, July 9, in Danville.

Because of several matters pending before Judge Michie in federal court which, if decided favorably, would release considerable bond money and drop hundreds of charges under both the injunction and the local ordinances of Danville, there had been division within the Movement. Some Movement people wanted to cease demonstrations by the dedicated, hard core of young people.

But Judge Michie's injunction against the Movement, plus the haste in which it had been granted to the *City Hall* forces, as contrasted with the deliberation given the matters asked for by the Movement lawyers to lighten the heavy hand of oppression, eliminated the federal courts as a deterrent to future demonstrations. Protests continued.

But instead of the previous mass action, it assumed the nature of strategic action reflecting more care in planning. At a mass meeting held at the Bibleway Church on the afternoon of July 4, 1963, it had been learned that Martin Luther King and the task force would arrive on July 11. The Reverend Lawrence Campbell had expressed the Movement's goal at that mass meeting:

"We're going to demonstrate! We're going to move!

"When Dr. King comes in here, we want Danville hot!"

Ivanhoe Donaldson, SNCC field secretary who shuttled between organizing and leading protest marches in nearby Prince Edward County, Va. (where the schools had been closed for four years) and demonstrating and getting arrested in Danville—had done research in the library at the New York Stock exchange, consulted Moody's *Industrials* and industrial directories for Virginia to learn as much about the ownership and operation of Dan River Mills as those sources provided. Based on this research he encouraged the Movement to call for a national boycott of the products of the Dan River Mills until the Mill used its economic power over Danville to cause an end to segregation. Cessation of the racial practices within the Dan River Mills plants were then projected as part of the Movement goals.

"Hit and Run" direct action squads were formed. These were small groups of students who would suddenly appear at a restaurant and conduct a sit-in and leave before the police arrived, or stretch out in front of Dan River Mills gates when workers were changing shifts and cause traffic tie-ups. Codes were worked out by them for use on tapped telephones and their operations were so secret that the adult leadership only learned about demonstrations from the radio news. Nonviolent guerrilla warfare best describes their tactics.

Herbert Coulton, SCLC Virginia voter-registration expert, got his machinery rolling after several weeks of training volunteer help and canvassing the Negro communities. On his first day set for beginning the actual registration, July 8, fifty-six persons were registered, a record for Danville's voter registration office. (Some appreciation for the magnitude of this task is gained from knowing how one must go about registering. The applicant is given a blank sheet of paper and required, without aids, to write the answers to ten questions such as date of birth and the place of residence and occupation *"for one year next preceding"* the date of application . . . without having the questions in front of him. Va. Code 24-68.)

On July 9, 1963, the hearing was held by Judge Michie in Danville to get the federal injunction against the Movement dissolved. Laden with the legal memoranda and opinions and order dissolving the Albany, Ga., federal injunction, Bill Kunstler and Art Kinoy urged voiding of the groundless order. Judge Michie refused, and took the matter under advisement. Having gone through the procedure of asking Judge Michie to dissolve his own injunction and been denied immediate relief, the delay while Judge Michie took the matter under advisement could be disregarded. They flew to Baltimore to appear before the Honorable Simon E. Sobeloff, Chief Judge of the United States Court of Appeals for the Fourth Circuit (it has jurisdiction over appeals from U.S. District Courts in Maryland, Virginia, North Carolina, West Virginia, and South Carolina). Simultaneously notice was given attorneys John Carter and James A. Ferguson. The depth of the legal team in skill and numbers finally tired the two *City Hall* lawyers. Carter and Ferguson notified Chief Judge Sobeloff they would not attend the hearing appealing the federal injunction issued by Judge Michie. In short order, Chief Judge Sobeloff called Judge Michie. On the evening of July 10, Michie dissolved the federal injunction . . . a minor victory for the Movement . . . whose "sweet taste" was denied for the most part by the companion action taken.

The cases of those charged with violating the Corporation Court injunction, all 105 of us were remanded to the Corporation Court . . . as sit-ins, picketing of Dan River Mills and blocking of its gates, and more Negroes became registered voters. The City had become "hot" for the arrival of King and the task force.

On Thursday, July 11, 1963, Dr. Martin Luther King arrived in Danville fresh from tours across the United States, where he had been received by tens of thousands in several of the major cities as the symbol of the Birmingham racial protests which had so aroused the nation to the plight of the southern Negroes and Negroes in general. More than 75,000 persons appeared as his audience in Los Angeles and contributed in excess of $50,000 to the work of SCLC. In Cleveland, traffic in a 10-block area had become jammed as the people poured forth to hear King. In Detroit 250,-000 had marched down Woodward Avenue behind King and given $50,000 in support. At the moment King arrived in Danville on July 11 there was probably only one living American who could have attracted larger gatherings: the late President John F. Kennedy. The Negroes in Danville had been "buked, beaten, betrayed, and scorned" but now there was a new day aborn.

As King arrived waves of students marched downtown and some sixty were arrested, including Miss Annie Pearl Avery of SNCC. The word of his presence was spread throughout Danville and thousands came to the High Street Baptist Church that night, cramming their bodies into every conceivable bit of space to hear his message. The seats in the main auditorium, balcony, Sunday School auditorium, and the aisle around them were filled with Negroes whose souls thirsted for the inspiration of his leadership, his presence, and his voice. Accompanying him was his faithful and able aid from the days of the Montgomery Bus Boycott of 1956: the Reverend Ralph Abernathy.

The temperature was in the 90's outside the church. Inside the television lights and human bodies jammed together made it hotter, but not a person cared. The parade of lesser personages in the hierarchy of the Danville Movement and SCLC whetted appetites for King even more. Just before King spoke, the Reverend Abernathy made the plea for money in order that the Movement's work could go on. About $4,000 was collected—mostly from the seasonal tobacco workers and the domestics who were willing to make another sacrifice if it would help that better day come.

While the program went on in the main auditorium, the SNCC and CORE staff members assigned to Danville were making plans for a night demonstration. With the arrival of Dr. King the national press, which had forsaken Danville, finding nothing spectacular about the routine arrests and demonstrations, had returned. It was hoped that King would lead the demonstration.

King delivered a stirring oration that night. He gave renewed hope. Near the end of the address he hurtled into the audience the remarks and challenge, "Walk together, children. Walk together, children and don't you get weary. There's a mighty camp meeting in the promised land." "We Shall Overcome" was sung and lines of marchers formed downstairs. The CORE and SNCC staff members asked Dr. King to lead the march to City Hall. The hour was close to 11:00 P.M. and hot. King had told the audience, "We will be with you until this problem is solved and injunctions can't stop a Movement." The request to lead the march to City Hall was politely turned down; giving the sickly condition of his stomach and the pressing need for his presence in New York to help plan the forthcoming *March on Washington* as his reasons.

More than two-hundred persons marched from the church to City Hall where a mighty army of police and state troopers were poised with clubs in hand and coupled fire hoses had the pressure up. Chief McCain's voice boomed forth over the midnight silence of the business area: "Git on back where you came from!" Hundreds of the demonstrators fled. Thirteen—including the Reverend Lendell Chase, the Reverend Virgil Wood, who headed the Lynchburg SCLC, and Matthew Jones of SNCC's staff—stood their ground and were arrested.

This marked the beginning of what appeared to be a *jail-in*—a form of pressuring a community to meet some of the demands by forcing the community to assume costs of feeding and housing far more prisoners than the local budgets or facilities can handle.

On the following day, June 12, the demonstrations continued with more arrests each day. Almost all of those arrested remained in jail. There had been a hearing set before the United States Court of Appeals for the Fourth Circuit for July 16. When the legal staff wasn't in court defending those recently arrested, visiting them in jail, or answering hundreds of questions, the time was spent preparing for the Baltimore hearing.

Dr. King had informed the Negroes of Danville: "You have my full personal support and the support of the Southern Christian Leadership Conference." "We're not afraid of jails. You've got to march and fill up the Danville jails." "We've got to have strong, massive, nonviolent demonstrations in Danville until the city engages in good faith negotiations with Negroes about their equal rights." His remarks had their effect as each day more and more persons demonstrated . . . and were arrested.

For the hearing in Baltimore the work had been divided. Part was being done by Kunstler and Kinoy in New York; the other part was performed by those of us in Danville. Coming to our aid was Richard Goodman of the Detroit law firm of Goodman, Crockett, Eden, Robb and Philo. Sunday, July 13, Goodman and I left for Washington, D.C., where we engaged in research and another all-night session in a frantic effort to have a brief ready for July 16. We were joined in this effort by Shelley Bowers and Phil Hirschkop, two "D.C." lawyers.

When the hearings began before Chief Judge Simon Sobeloff and his associate, the Honorable Albert V. Bryan, on June 16, 1963, there were 140 persons staying in jails without bail. Some of them had been shipped to the jails of nearby communities. Among those in jail was Buford Holt, the demonstrating G.I. from Ft. Bragg, who had picketed Mayor Julian R. Stinson's house along with several others and carried the American Flag while in uniform.

Hopes were high for the hearing before Chief Judge Sobeloff, who enjoys the reputation of being one of the most eminent legal scholars alive. We stated the facts, argued the law and participated in a closed discussion in his chambers in which he encouraged both sides of the Danville dispute to consider negotiations. The lawyers for the Movement—all nine of us—indicated that we thought our clients would agree to this. Councilman John Carter was adamant: "No!"

The appearance before the United States Court of Appeals for the Fourth Circuit, our first one, ended without a quick decision. We were told to submit more briefs, which were to be filed by both sides within ten days. Back in Danville we learned that there had been an announcement of no demonstrations until Judge Sobeloff had ruled, that the mass meeting had been addressed by one of the south's leading white integrationists, Mrs. Anne Braden, editor of the *Southern Patriot,* that sixteen white ministers in Danville had petitioned the City Hall for a biracial committee and that one of the sixteen ministers, Dr. Cecil Robert Taylor, had already been asked to resign . . . and the promised SCLC task force hadn't arrived . . . yet.

The announcement of no demonstrations remained in effect until Saturday, July 20, 1963, when seventy-eight-year-old Dan McCain got arrested again for picketing along with Mrs. Anne Karro, fifty-three and white, and several others. Mrs. Karro was from Bethesda, Md. Bond on each of the adults was placed at $2,500.

Because there were few people being arrested and because there were no trials of the injunction cases in Corporation Court, many of the normal business hours of the Movement lawyers were spent handling cases in Juvenile Court that had been continued again and again. *City Hall* was proceeding with greater caution at this point.

The lack of trials of the persons accused of violating the injunction flowed from fear of what might be done by the Court of Appeals, which had the validity of the Corporation Court injunction as one of the matters under consideration. Days were easier now. Richard Goodman had returned to Detroit and local lawyers were getting eight hours' sleep.

Meanwhile the attempt to boycott Dan River Mills gained steam. Bill Mahoney of SNCC, along with Cleveland Robinson of District 65 in New York, had arranged picketing of the New York office of Dan River Mills. Enough concern was created so that Malcom Cross of the Mill arranged a conference with the Reverend Lawrence G. Campbell and Mrs. Beatrice Hairston of the Movement on July 22, 1963. There were no more such conferences.

Those in the "jail-in" were still there on July 23, 1963. The Movement was now projecting a "D-Day" operation, a massive march of people on a planned occasion. Danville's "D-Day" was the mental projection of Wyatt Walker, Martin Luther King's chief assistant, who lingered around Danville for a couple of days during the latter part of July. "D-Day" was the imposition of Wyatt's 1963 Birmingham protest thinking on the Danville situation by a mind that had forgotten that "D-Day" hadn't produced meaningful results in Albany, Ga., the year before in 1962. Large numbers were supposed to march on one day and fill the Danville jails. In Birmingham in 1963 "Bull" Connor's jails had been filled and he had no means of spreading the prisoners throughout the state of Alabama. As could Albany, Ga., Danville could send its prisoners to every place for incarceration operated in Virginia.

But things were altered slightly. On the afternoon of July 23, 1963, Tuesday, word was received from the United States Court of Appeals that there would be no decision forthcoming until after there had been a hearing September

23, 1963, of the Danville matters before the Court of Appeals by all five Judges who are members of that Court.

A blow was struck. The green light was given. The Corporation Court made plans to proceed with trials of some 370 persons charged with violating the injunction. Those identified with *City Hall* chortled their approval of the United States Court of Appeals. At the Movement headquarters on Union Street and the office of Harvey and Wood on South Main things were glum . . . very glum.

On July 25, 1963, Thursday, it looked as if the "ship" had really sprung a leak. The Reverend Lendell Chase, by reason of his consistent demonstrating, was coming to be looked upon as the symbol of the Danville Movement. Julius Adams never did any self-projection; he just worked at whatever tasks the Movement assigned, pulled his night shift at Dan River Mills, contributed part of his paycheck to the Movement, and looked and hoped for the day that the SCLC task force, or somebody, or something, would deliver a victory. The Reverend Alexander I. Dunlap ceased to be an operative force of any importance in the Movement leadership; most of his time was now being spent in Kittrell, N.C., where he was to assume duties as Vice-President of Kittrell College. Campbell had become a paid administrator of the Movement and his tasks were mundane, unspectacular, necessarily and deliberately designed to minimize the possibility of further arrests of him. Hence, the symbolic role was left to the Reverend Chase.

Chase had been in jail since the night of July 11, 1963, the date of Dr. King's visit to Danville enroute to New York. Fifteen days later, July 25, 1963, Chase, his wife, and his daughter were bailed out of jail, leaving absent one hundred other demonstrators carrying on the "jail-in." Some of those remaining in jail understood, others didn't; all found his leaving a bit discouraging and the situation was not helped by the continued failure of the SCLC Task Force to arrive. Only after visits to the jail by Campbell and his announcement that "D-Day" was scheduled for Sunday, July 28, 1963, did the morale of those jailed restore itself—somewhat. Annie Pearl Avery, inside jail, gave a needed assist.

Few knew it, but a real crisis existed. It was not a question of "jail without bail." There was no bail money. Local sources for bonding people had been dried up and the SCLC office in Atlanta was not responding to the pleas of bond money from the leaders of the Danville Movement. As the pressures mounted from the hundreds of phone calls from concerned parents, spouses, and relatives, Campbell began calling almost hourly to the Atlanta SCLC screaming for bond money.

Knowledge of this crushed down upon the shoulders of the lawyers. "What good is our knowledge if those people remain in jail solely because they can't raise exorbitant bail?" we asked ourselves. Fred Findling supplied an answer.

Findling, a short, dapper, and soft-spoken lawyer with prematurely gray hair, down from his offices in the Cadillac Tower in Detroit for the week, initiated another all-night session of research, typing, and mimeographing. He was willing to try to apply directly to the Virginia Supreme Court of Appeals in a *Habeas Corpus* action. The statutes said it could be done, so we did it. After all, weren't our clients held illegally? The chances of success were remote, but anything was better than doing nothing.

"D-Day" was approaching. On July 27, 1963, Campbell had collected over 300 signed pledges "to march." He confidently predicted that as many as 1,000 persons *might* demonstrate on July 28. Somehow Campbell's optimism got to the press. The counter-response was the running of stories and pictures showing elaborate plans being made by Chief McCain for the arresting, transporting, and incarcerating of a thousand people in the jails and City Armory.

With the downtown section of Danville vacated and inundated with cops whose low murmurs pierced the Sunday afternoon quiet, the "D-Day" fiasco began. Some seventy-seven persons marched a couple of blocks before being arrested. Fifteen of the number were students from a privately supported Baptist College in Richmond, Union University. These students were accompanied to Danville by one of their professors, Ben-Zion Wardy, who was loaded with pounds of hamburger impregnated with aphrodisiac as a weapon against police dogs.

Shortly after 5:00, July 28, 1963, Bob Zellner was arrested again. He was a marked man and his presence in a crowd of reporters watching the demonstration was enough to establish complicity and guilt in the minds of the violent whites of Danville. Morale had been shattered further by the lack of numbers . . . in the "D-Day" demonstration.

At the mass meeting at Bibleway Church later that day there was no "mass." A desperate effort was made to bolster sagging spirits. Six volunteers were requested for a sit-in. Three ladies raised their hands. The minister presiding asked, "Won't a man come forward?" Avon Rollins commented, "Ain't none in here."

The "Dee" in "D-Day" could have well been for *damned*. The police terror was so complete that people could no longer be brought to demonstrate. Ninety to 99 per cent of the bonds and operating expenses for bail, court reporters, transcripts, supplies, and other matters came from the pockets of the Negro community whose median income was a mere $2,578 (the national median income for Negroes is $3,233). At this point the Negroes of Danville were "bankrupt."

Only isolated acts of desperation and legal decisions which could soften blows were within the realm of possibility. Campbell continued his insistent calls for bail money for the nearly 200 persons in jail. These calls to Atlanta had to be made collect. Recriminations erupted in the situation of hopelessness. The SNCC and CORE staff members, who handled the actual implementation of the direct action protest, began to express openly to the Movement leaders their objections to carrying out the plans of others (Campbell, Chase, Wyatt T. Walker) who seemed not to know what they were doing. The "D-Day" operation was a case in point. SNCC and CORE had opposed the notion. They had no faith that large numbers would be gotten and knew that all the jails in Virginia could never be filled. Further objection was with regard to the day. "Why march downtown on a day that there is no one there to observe or to become concerned because they won't be there to be inconvenienced?" They wanted "D-Day" held, if it must be held, during the busiest part of a day when more shoppers would be around.

On the afternoon of July 28, 1963, Erwin Miller of Philadelphia came into town to work with Jerry Williams and Miss Ruth Harvey in the hearing on whether to make the Corporation Court injunction permanent.

Because the Corporation Court was being utilized on July 29 for the hearing to make the injunction permanent, there were no trials set for those charged with violating the injunction. George Downing of Detroit came in under the auspices of the Guild's CLAS program to replace Fred

Findling. All hands were busy in the Municipal and Juvenile Courts.

Rush was upon us. More help was needed. As soon as the hearings finished on making the Corporation Court injunction permanent, trials of those accused of violating that injunction would begin in earnest. Through William Higgs of Washington, several workers were recruited: Jack Oppenheim and Bert Pogrebin came to Danville from New York; Miss Ann Cooper flew down from Boston.

Finally Atlanta SCLC came through. The Resolute Insurance Company of Hartford, Conn., came into town and began writing bails for the demonstrators, nearly 200 of them. A little of the tension released when this operation began on July 30, 1963. That day, out of desperation, a conference was held between the Commonwealth Attorney and the defense counsels. Our backs were pushed to the wall. Separate trials for the more than 300 persons on the injunction meant separate records, separate days of court reporters and time, time, time. And after conviction the amount of the bonds might go up. We pressed for something, anything. There was no bond money, no money for court reporters, no money for anything. Phone call after phone call and letters to King's office in Atlanta were ignored or we were told "SCLC is broke," as we thumbed through copies of *Jet* reporting on mammoth contributions.

The power structure of Danville was also anxious to get rid of the hundreds of cases—which, if tried individually as we had been insisting, and doing—would go on for four more years. Because 75 per cent of the persons charged were being represented by one lawyer, bringing in extra judges would provide little relief to the cluttering of the docket. After all, that one lawyer could only be in one courtroom before one judge at a time.

Fortunately, another conference was held, far away, in Detroit. Richard Goodman (who had just returned from Danville) discussed the plight of the Movement with regard to the injunction cases with Art Kinoy (who was in Detroit enroute to his home in New York) and George Crockett. After hearing a lot of discussion of the facts and the disappointment at the United States Court of Appeals for the Fourth Circuit denial of immediate stopping of the injunction trials and prosecution, Crockett asked a simple question:

"Have you filed a *written* motion with the Court of Appeals asking it to enjoin the prosecutions?" After learning that the answer was "No," Crockett suggested that one be filed. And it was filed on August 6, 1963. A hearing on the motion to stop prosecutions was set for August 8, 1963, in Baltimore.

Back in Danville on August 5, the 346 defendants charged with violating the injunction crowded into Corporation Court and the roll was called. After the filing of several new defense motions, which were not ruled on immediately, the Commonwealth Attorney, Eugene Link, did what for him in these cases was a strange thing: he filed a motion. That motion was shortly granted by Judge Aiken. It called for the transfer of more than 200 of the cases to courts scattered across Virginia. One of the nearest communities where a case was sent to be tried was 80 miles away. The farthest place was Virginia Beach, approximately 250 miles away.

This move to transfer the Danville cases was a misapplication of a statute, Va. 19.1-224. This statute was designed to permit the transfer of a case from one community to another change of venue, when there were strong community feelings of a type which would prevent the accused from getting a *fair* trial in the community. The Danville Commonwealth Attorney, Eugene Link, asserted that the cases should be transferred because the crowded docket of the Danville court would not permit a *speedy* trial inasmuch as the 346 defendants were all insisting on their right to individual trials by juries. The right to a speedy trial is the right of the accused. In Danville at that time the accused persons didn't assert their right to a speedy trial; all were willing to wait their turn.

On its face the move was frightening. Either the demonstrators had to give up their right to an individual trial or be impoverished further by having to travel hundreds of miles and transport their witnesses those same hundreds of miles. It also meant pressure on the lawyers, who conceivably would have to travel thousands of miles crisscrossing the state 300 miles from one end to the other end on succeeding days. On the face of it the move was, indeed, frightening. One Movement leader's reaction was understandable: "This Court is but a different kind of policeman's club."

City Hall gloated. They knew that it would be a long time before surging black Danville citizens would pour into the streets again singing "Freedom"; *City Hall* knew that little money trickled in from the headquarters of SCLC to underwrite the expenses of the Danville protest; *City Hall* knew that the local lawyers, who had served so long, under an exhaustive schedule, had been given *evasion* instead of money to pay the mounting legal expenses; *City Hall* knew that more and more of the demonstrators had lost jobs as the almost daily roll calls had been forced upon the demonstrators even when the cases were technically in the sole power of the local United States District Court. *City Hall* knew this and more because telephones were tapped.

But the smirks soon disappeared. On August 8 in

Baltimore Art Kinoy, Jerry Williams, Ruth Harvey, and Bill Kunstler presented the request for a stay of the prosecutions. The raw, naked power displayed in transferring the cases hundreds of miles away was so shocking that the conservative members of the Court of Appeals were aroused at last. Led by Chief Judge Simon Sobeloff, the United States Court of Appeals entered an immediate order banning all further trials of those 346 charged with violating the Aiken injunction. Strangely, only the trials were enjoined or banned; arrests could still be made under the law—but no trials. The Danville Movement was so starved for vindication and encouragement that the fact that all wasn't gotten didn't disturb them too much, if at all.

The response of the Negro community was immediate and dramatic. That night some 2,000 persons . . . second in attendance only to the mass meeting where Dr. King had spoken a month before . . . turned out stomped their feet, sang their songs, shouted their joy, paraded up and down the aisles, and literally poured forth a wellspring of emotions for seven solid hours in the High Street Baptist Church. Dramatically the meeting closed with Jerry Williams making a few remarks and presenting Ruth Harvey who had just flown from the hearings in Baltimore with him. In tearful eloquence Ruth read the full text of the order of the United States Court of Appeals for the Fourth Circuit.

When news of the order was hinted in Danville, the three courts (Corporation, Municipal and Juvenile) closed shop on the demonstration cases and the three judges began a vacation delayed by the hundreds of cases.

With the court in vacation and prosecution of injunction charges enjoined, I was free to leave Danville. A long fall from a high building had ended.

Tired, and broke, on August 9, 1963, I packed a change

of clothing, maalox tablets, and a copy of the *Liberator* magazine and joined George Downing on the drive to the Danville airport and a flight north. All thoughts of pending trials, appeals, jails, and penitentiaries were thrust into my subconsciousness. I rode on that plane as light in spirit as the clouds through which its wings knifed at 200 miles per hour . . . towards the National Airport of Washington, D.C.

A summer had ended.

An experience had concluded.

CHAPTER 15

After the Fact

> *Hold fast to dreams*
> *For if dreams die*
> *Life is a broken-winged bird*
> *That cannot fly.*
>
> *Hold fast to dreams*
> *For when dreams go*
> *Life is a barren field*
> *Frozen with snow.*
> —Langston Hughes, "Dreams"

In September of 1963 the killing of six Negro children in Birmingham and the March on Washington had faded slightly in the memories of the 47,000 residents of Danville.

The Movement had completed a full circle as Jack Greenberg's NAACP Legal Defense Fund (which was so unacceptable in June when the Movement was demonstration-minded), was brought in and began handling some of the minor cases (charges such as trespass, resisting arrest, parading without a permit were involved) not covered by the injunction of August 8, 1963, of the U.S. Court of Appeals for the Fourth Circuit.

Out of a sense of practicality and desperation, the insistence on individual trials for individuals was abandoned;

in flotsam-like-groupings these charges were tried in Corporation Court where fines as high as $50.00 and sentences of up to twenty days were meted out on each of the 265 charges, with part of the sentence suspended upon condition of good behavior for two years. The sentences were appealed to the highest court of Virginia, the Court of Appeals, where they are still pending. Assertions were still being made: "The task force is coming."

In Richmond, Va., on September 22, 1963, the national convention of SCLC attracted 600 delegates and hundreds of guests who listened to a glowing report from the treasurer, the Reverend Dr. Ralph Abernathy, who announced that more than $800,000 had been raised and that there was a "surplus" in excess of $200,000.

At the same convention Martin Luther King called for an intensified rights drive and massive demonstrations "with Danville as one of our main targets."

On the following day, September 23, 1963, Art Kinoy and Bill Kunstler (before the U.S. Court of Appeals for the Fourth Circuit) again met in battle their equally tired opponents from Danville, Councilman John Carter and City Attorney James Ferguson. They argued the merits of the relief sought and denied in the U.S. District Court of Danville.

In October of 1963, Andrew Young of King's SCLC again announced to the press ". . . the task force is coming to Danville." The realities of Danville had not yet been discerned by SCLC as Young spoke: "Despite demonstrations and racial troubles in Danville for most of the summer, nothing was really accomplished. It took us a month to prepare Birmingham for demonstrations and we are going to begin that process in Danville."

The promise was renewed again in November of 1963

when Wyatt T. Walker of the SCLC Atlanta staff came to Danville and talked about more demonstrations and stated: "We are prepared to stay until the job is done." Four days later, November 15, 1963, five of the nine members of the Danville City Council met with the leadership of the Danville Movement, C. T. Vivian of SCLC and Jack Greenberg and Sam Tucker of the NAACP Legal Defense Fund. At this time the old split between the Danville SCLC and the Danville NAACP was again open and notorious, so the five councilmen announced a future meeting with the Danville NAACP. (The Danville NAACP had not been invited to the original meeting.) Councilman John Carter, who refused to meet with the Negroes and their one white ally, Jack Greenberg, was furious. Carter soon used this meeting for lethal political purposes.

The evening of November 15, 1963, Martin Luther King, one of America's greatest orators, spoke at Danville's High Street Baptist Church with the same impelling message of *Freedom Now* he used on August 28, 1963, to enthrall millions at the March on Washington and those who viewed it on television.

Where on July 11, 1963, there had been thousands of Negroes crowding, sardine-fashion, into the huge facilities of High Street, there were less than 500 present on November 15. For some reason, Danville's Negroes honored King's presence with their absence. It was a Friday night. Perhaps there was a television special showing.

In November the vaunted SCLC "task force" arrived. After many desperate tries at mobilization, the *message* got across.

King's "task force" left.

It was too late. A summer of hope had ended.

The cases of the 346 persons charged with violating the Danville Corporation Court injunction are still pending before the United States Court of Appeals for the Fourth Circuit althugh eighteen months have passed as of the date of this writing. Each of the 346 persons must make the possibility of an adverse ruling by the U.S. Court of Appeals part of all plans. One day, any day, they may be required to go and stand trial on the charge of violating the injunction in a Danville court.

As of the date of this writing, the trials of the fourteen persons charged with violation of the John Brown law has not been held. Each, like myself, is out of jail on a $5,000 bond. The death of a federal judge, crowded calendar of the federal courts, and other matters have caused this delay.

Just as the persons awaiting trials are inconvenienced, so are the more than 200 local persons inconvenienced who placed their homes as security for the $300,000 in bail needed to free those charged with violating the injunction and the John Brown law.

During the spring of 1964 while the civil rights forces in Mississippi headed by SNCC were mobilizing 1,000 volunteers from the north to come and operate Freedom Schools, Community Centers, and conduct voter registration as part of a year round program in Mississippi, Dr. King and his SCLC task force began their preparation for the several weeks of massive nonviolent onslaught in America's oldest segregated city, St. Augustine.

But the handwriting was on the many walls.

The tactic of massive, block-buster, blunderbuss marching of black bodies down hot southern streets (which appeared to succeed so well in Birmingham, and perhaps St. Augustine, and appeared to fail dismally in Albany and

Danville) will be of limited value in the coming years except as a "shocker" to begin community organization and overcome social inertia.

THE WHITE FOLKS

At first one is tempted to call the protest in Danville during the summer of 1963 a struggle for "Negro Freedom," but it was more. The facts indicate that the lack of Freedom crossed color lines.

There was almost total silence by the more than 33,000 white citizens of Danville during that summer because those white citizens were not free. A professional man of the community—who must even at this date go unnamed because of the real danger of reprisal—wasn't free to bring Negroes through the front door of the office; he'd sneak them through a side door.

When the sixteen leading white ministers suggested openly that a Negro ought to be a part of the committee working on a solution to the "racial" problem the reaction in their churches was violent. One was dismissed forthwith. The others were censured.

Five members of the City Council who defied Councilman John Carter, by merely talking with Movement leaders, were summarily voted out of office. The limitations of speech were not limited to racial matters alone. In September of 1964 a lone member of the large audience attending the meeting of the City Democratic Committee made a motion that the group "hold its nose" and endorse President Lyndon Johnson. The motion never got a second and the maker of the motion was threatened.

The more than 33,000 white citizens of Danville speak

with one voice, the voice and viewpoint of John W. Carter—or else.

If Danville's Negroes had been successful in breaking open the walls of the prison during the summer of 1963, their white inmates also could have escaped.

SPECIFICS OF DANVILLE

If this book prods gods, shakes a few fictions, and tarnishes a myth or two, as it poses the question of where we, who dare to dream, can go from here—well and good. But the question of specific achievement cannot well be avoided. One could say, as W. E. B. Du Bois did, that agitation is good in the sense of a toothache that warns of the presence of disease, for if one doesn't cry out when corruption visits his body he may suffer death. Far worse than death is the silence that makes the suffering of a man unfathomable to his fellow men. There was agitation in Danville, agitation which should only be viewed as a small symptom of a larger problem. There are a few positive specifics and many negative ones such as the efficient way the John Carter-led forces saw to it in June of 1964 that the five city councilmen who held a conference with the Movement leaders on November 15, 1963, were defeated. In an eleventh hour radio appeal to voters, Carter told the citizenry that Danville faced "grave dangers" if it re-elected a group of men willing to negotiate with "communist-influenced agitators."

One of the best products of the Danville Summer of Protest was a lesson of how lawyers can best relate to large-scale civil rights efforts. George Crockett and Ernie Goodman of the Guild's CLAS took the Danville legal organization structure to Mississippi during the summer of 1964 as did Jack Greenberg of the NAACP. The Danville approach of rotating teams of northern lawyers under the supervision of civil rights veterans on the scene, backed by groups elsewhere handling the detailed legal research and appeals, was employed extensively in SNCC's Mississippi Freedom Summer Project. And so was the *Kunstler Statute,* whose use in Danville stimulated the inclusion of Title IX in the 1964 Civil Rights Bill. Almost all of the arrests during the 1964 Mississippi project were taken to federal courts of Mississippi from state courts.

Not only were some of the legal procedures and organizational arrangements taken to Mississippi by those lawyers who had participated in Danville, but almost all of the lawyers themselves on the Mississippi scene during 1964 were enriched by their Danville experiences: George Crockett, Jack Greenberg, George Downing, Arthur Kinoy, William Kunstler, Erwin Miller, Ann Cooper, Bert Pogrebin, Ernie Goodman, Phil Hirschkop, Harry Lore, Jack Oppenheim, and the "Snake Doctor."

There are other specifics—but there aren't many:
one Negro policeman hired;
desegregation of the 315-bed Memorial Hospital;
passage of a fair employment ordinance in city jobs
    (public not private);
registration of 800-plus new Negro voters;
employment of several Negro persons in sales positions.

One should not be disturbed that the specifics are so few in light of the history of Danville—a typical one-judge, two-industry town where there are families that traditionally rule and others who have been traditionally ruled.

In 1963 Negroes tried to move Danville . . . and failed.

Labor unions attempted to move the intransigent *heart* of the town when 4,000 textile workers struck in 1931. They struck the booming industry again in 1951. These were white men fighting for better wages, working conditions and the recognition of their union. Both times the efforts of the textile workers met with frustration as they were opposed by the same police who brutalized the Negroes and National Guardsmen. Little wonder that the Negroes did not meet more success.

For the most part the Danville textile workers are complacent members of a complacent textile workers union who consider themselves well off. They achieved this perspective by comparing their life with a standard: the living conditions and wages of the Negroes of Danville. The Negro is both their standard and their *enemy*. Realizing this, they are told by *City Hall* that Negroes are trying to force their way into the union and thus destroy the seniority rights of the white members and their right to pass on their trades to their sons, along with forcing their daughters to sit beside Negro children in the public schools.

The Danville Movement fought alone clinging to the hope that Martin Luther King or the federal government would forestall an ugly resolution of matters.

The Movement fought the same forces as those which fought the textile workers. Racial segregation made the Negroes bystanders and potential "scabs," during the two organizational efforts of the textile workers. That same racism kept the white textile workers in a neutral—if not hostile—position as the Negroes sought a better life in 1963.

It is difficult not to believe that different results would have been achieved if both the white textile workers and the Negroes had joined hands against a common foe.

So much for the specifics.

The fourteen persons yet awaiting trial and possible imprisonment, the hundreds facing jailings for shorter periods, and the thousands who supported their efforts, did not respond from considerations of "specific achievements" or "Victory." We responded when the questions of "specifics" or "victory" were morally irrelevant. We responded in spite of our fears—in desperation—in the only way that our consciences would permit: to contain beasts that roamed Danville in the guise of men, mauling black citizens and intimidating the few questioning white citizens.

Ours was an act of conscience.

Appendix

TITLE 18, U.S. CODE, SECTION 241
CONSPIRACY AGAINST RIGHTS OF CITIZENS

If two or more persons conspire to injure, oppress, threaten, or intimidate any citizen in the free exercise or enjoyment of any right or privilege secured to him by the Constitution or laws of the United States, or because of his having so exercised the same; or

If two or more persons go in disguise on the highway, or on the premises of another, with intent to prevent or hinder his free exercise or enjoyment of any right or privilege so secured—

They shall be fined not more than $5,000 or imprisoned not more than ten years, or both. (June 25, 1948, ch. 645, 62 Stat. 696.)

TITLE 18, U.S. CODE, SECTION 242
DEPRIVATION OF RIGHTS UNDER COLOR OF LAW

Whoever, under color of any law, statute, ordinance, regulation, or custom, wilfully subjects any inhabitant of any State, Territory, or District to the deprivation of any rights, privileges, or immunities secured or protected by the Constitution or laws of the United States, or to different punishments, pains, or penalties, on account of such inhabitant being an alien, or by reason of his color, or race, than are prescribed for the punishment of citizens, shall be fined not more than $1,000 or imprisoned not more than one year, or both. (June 25, 1948, ch. 645, 62 Stat. 696.)

DANVILLE CORPORATION COURT INJUNCTION

This day came the plaintiff, by Counsel, and presented to the Court its motion for a temporary injunction and restraining order, which motion was verified and upon the presentation and consideration of said verified motion and affidavit of T. Edward Temple, City Manager of the City of Danville;

Upon due consideration whereof it appearing to the Court that the plaintiff herein is entitled to the temporary injunction and restraining order prayed for and that under the circumstances of this case, no notice to said named defendants herein is necessary or practicable, it is ADJUDGED, ORDERED and DECREED as follows:

1. That said named defendants, their servants, agents and employees, their attorneys and all other persons acting in concert therewith be, and they hereby are, enjoined and restrained until the further order of this Court from participating in the following actions or conduct:

(a) Unlawfully assembling in an unauthorized manner on the public streets and in the vicinity of the public buildings of the City of Danville;

(b) Unlawful interference with the lawful operation of private enterprises and businesses in the City of Danville;

(c) Unlawfully obstructing the freedom of movement of the general public of the City of Danville and the general traffic of the City of Danville;

(d) Unlawfully obstructing the entrances and exits to and from both private business concerns and public facilities in the City of Danville;

(e) Participating in and inciting mob violence, rioting and inciting persons to rioting;

(f) Unlawfully carrying deadly weapons, threatening to use said deadly weapons, assaulting divers citizens in this community;

(g) Unlawfully using loud and boisterous language interrupting the peace and repose of the citizens of the community, business establishments of the community and the public works of the community;

(h) Creating and maintaining a public nuisance by reason of unlawful and unauthorized gatherings and loud, boisterous and concerted demonstrations interfering with the peace and quiet and enjoyment of the citizens of the City of Danville.

2. This temporary injunction and restraining order shall be effective immediately and shall continue from day to day until the further order of this Court until July 6, 1963, at which time it shall stand dissolved unless prior thereto it be enlarged or further temporary or permanent injunction granted herein.

3. And that a copy of this Order be served upon the named defendants herein.

TITLE 28, U.S. CODE, SECTION 1443

"Any of the following civil actions or criminal prosecutions, commenced in a State court may be removed by the defendant to the district court of the United States for the district and division embracing the place wherein it is pending:

"(1) Against any person who is denied or cannot enforce in the courts of such State a right under any law providing for the equal civil rights of citizens of the United States, or of all persons within the jurisdiction thereof;

"(2) For any act under color of authority derived from any law providing for equal rights, or for refusing to do any act on the ground that it would be inconsistent with such law."

TITLE 9, 1964 CIVIL RIGHTS BILL, INTERVENTION AND
PROCEDURE AFTER REMOVAL IN CIVIL RIGHTS
CASES

Sec. 901. Title 28 of the United States Code, section 1447
(d), is amended to read as follows:

"An order remanding a case to the State court from which
it was removed is not reviewable on appeal or otherwise, except
that an order remanding a case to the State court from which
it was removed pursuant to section 1443 of this title shall be
reviewable by appeal or otherwise."

Sec. 902. Whenever an action has been commenced in any
court of the United States seeking relief from the denial of equal
protection of the laws under the fourteenth amendment to the
Constitution on account of race, color, religion, or national origin,
the Attorney General for or in the name of the United States
may intervene in such action upon timely application if the Attorney General certifies that the case is of general public importance. In such action the United States shall be entitled to the
same relief as if it had instituted the action.

ORDINANCE NO. 63-6.2

AN ORDINANCE LIMITING PICKETING AND DEMONSTRATIONS;
PROVIDING PUNISHMENT FOR VIOLATIONS THEREOF

WHEREAS, large, noisy, lawless and rioting groups of
people, there being among these armed persons with records as
habitual criminals, under the pretext of picketing, have incited
racial strife, caused personal injuries and destruction of property; and,

WHEREAS, such groups have further disrupted the peace
and convenience of this community, have placed the citizenry in

Appendix 233

fear of its safety and have disrupted the orderly flow of both vehicular and pedestrian traffic; and,

WHEREAS, there are reasonable restraints which must be imposed upon freedom of speech and assembly when such freedoms are exercised in such a manner as to endanger the personal safety and property of the citizenry; and,

WHEREAS, it is necessary to impose reasonable regulations upon assemblies and picketing,

NOW, THEREFORE, BE IT ORDAINED, as follows:

(1) All assemblies and picketing shall be peaceful and unattended by noise and boisterousness, and there shall be no shouting, clapping or singing of such a nature as to disturb the peace and tranquility of the community; and,

(2) That marching shall be in single file and pickets or demonstrators shall be spaced a distance of not less than ten feet apart, and not more than six pickets shall picket or demonstrate before any given place of business or public facility; and,

(3) That all picketing or demonstrating shall be during the business or work hours of the place of business or public facility being picketed, and upon such days as such facility may be open for the transaction of business; and,

(4) That no picketing or demonstrating shall be performed within any public building; and,

(5) That no person under the age of eighteen years shall be permitted to march, picket or demonstrate in the City; and,

(6) That no vehicles shall be used in any picket or demonstrating line, and that all picketers or demonstrators shall be afoot; and,

(7) That violation of the foregoing regulations shall constitute a misdemeanor, and be punished as provided in Section 1-6 of the Code of the City of Danville, 1962.

COURT OF APPEALS OPINION
Before SOBELOFF, Chief Judge, and HAYNSWORTH and
J. SPENCER BELL, Circuit Judges.

PER CURIAM.

We are entering this order, for the reasons stated in it, to protect the jurisdiction of this court. It may be hoped, however, that the interval between now and September 23rd may be utilized by persons of good will of both races to establish communications and to seek eventually acceptable solutions to these problems out of which these cases arise. As long as the problems exist, courts will be called upon to adjudicate disputed rights associated with them, but the basic problems themselves can be resolved only by the people concerned.

ORDER

These matters came on for hearing upon the motion of the plaintiffs for an order restraining and enjoining the prosecution of all proceedings in any of the state courts of Virginia for alleged violations of Ordinance No. 63-6.2 of the City of Danville, Virginia, and for contempt arising out of alleged violations of the injunctive orders, temporary and permanent, passed on June 6, 1963, and August 3, 1963, by the Corporation Court of the City of Danville, Virginia, in the matter of the City of Danville, Virginia, versus Campbell, et al.

The plaintiffs in the District Court challenged the constitutionality of the ordinance and the temporary injunction order, mentioned above. Meanwhile some of the criminal prosecutions founded upon the ordinance were removed to the District Court. Thereafter the District Court refused the requested injunctive relief and remanded to the state court the removed criminal proceedings. The plaintiffs by appeal seek to review of the District Court's order in all of these cases.

In support of the plaintiff's motion for emergency relief, affidavits have been filed showing that all the criminal proceedings have been set for trial and one or more have been tried. Earlier, when several persons had been convicted and sentenced to effective jail terms of 45-90 days, they had been denied bail in the state court pending appeal, making impossible effective appellate review in the state courts of the constitutionality of the injunction and ordinance. Moreover, present trial and conviction of others among the persons charged with violation of the ordinance and injunction would moot their appeals in this court if they are required to serve their sentences before these cases can be heard and determined in this court. Should some or all of them be granted bail after conviction and pending appeal, they would be put to the expense of an appeal through the state courts while the same constitutional questions are pending in this court. On the other hand, hasty trials, if the convicted defendants are to be released on bail pending appeal serve no obvious purpose in aid of necessary maintenance of law and order.

Even more burdensome to many of the plaintiffs is the fact that, over their objections, some of their contempt charges have been transferred to other courts of Virginia, some as much as 200 miles from Danville, to which they must go and transport their witnesses if they are to defend themselves. Under those circumstances there is no adequate legal remedy in the state courts which, if one existed, might stay our hand.

In these circumstances this court can tolerate neither an interference with proper functioning of law enforcement officers in the maintenance of the public peace of Danville nor the nullification of constitutional rights of persons charged with the violation of the ordinance and the injunctive orders of the Corporation Court of Danville by permitting trials and punishments to be inflicted before the challenges to the validity of said ordinance and injunctive orders can be adjudicated in the appeals pending in this court.

Under all of the circumstances it appears that temporary relief is necessary to protect the jurisdiction of this court pending disposition of the appeals before us and to avoid irreparable injury.

Upon consideration, after hearing counsel for the parties, it is this 8th day of August, 1963, ordered that Eugene Link, Commonwealth Attorney, and T. F. Tucker, Clerk, Corporation Court Danville, Virginia, and all persons acting in concert with them or by their authority are hereby restrained and enjoined from bringing to trial any person for the alleged violation of said ordinance of the City of Danville and the injunctive orders of the Corporation Court of the City of Danville until the determination of the above appeals which have been set for hearing at the term of this court beginning on the 23rd day of September next.

It is further ordered that either party may seek upon a proper showing any change or modification of this order that may be deemed necessary or just pending said hearing.